Cambridge Elements

Elements in Public Economics

edited by

Robin Boadway
Queen's University

Frank A. Cowell
The London School of Economics and Political Science

Massimo Florio
University of Milan

FAMILY TAXATION

Patricia Apps
University of Sydney

Ray Rees[†]
University of Munich and CESifo

CAMBRIDGE
UNIVERSITY PRESS

Shaftesbury Road, Cambridge CB2 8EA, United Kingdom

One Liberty Plaza, 20th Floor, New York, NY 10006, USA

477 Williamstown Road, Port Melbourne, VIC 3207, Australia

314–321, 3rd Floor, Plot 3, Splendor Forum, Jasola District Centre,
New Delhi – 110025, India

103 Penang Road, #05–06/07, Visioncrest Commercial, Singapore 238467

Cambridge University Press is part of Cambridge University Press & Assessment,
a department of the University of Cambridge.

We share the University's mission to contribute to society through the pursuit of
education, learning and research at the highest international levels of excellence.

www.cambridge.org
Information on this title: www.cambridge.org/9781009479325

DOI: 10.1017/9781108973007

When citing this work, please include a reference to the DOI 10.1017/9781108973007

First published 2025

A catalogue record for this publication is available from the British Library.

ISBN 978-1-009-47932-5 Hardback
ISBN 978-1-108-97267-3 Paperback
ISSN 2516-2276 (online)
ISSN 2516-2268 (print)

Family Taxation

Elements in Public Economics

DOI: 10.1017/9781108973007
First published online: April 2025

Patricia Apps
University of Sydney

Ray Rees[†]
University of Munich and CESifo

Author for correspondence: Patricia Apps, patricia.apps@sydney.edu.au

Abstract: This Element seeks to provide an in-depth survey of the papers written on the optimal taxation of the incomes of the members of family households, as opposed to households with just a single individual, over the period beginning with the early 1980s and ending in the late 2010s. This literature, solidly within the public finance tradition, is not large, and so the Element gives quite a full exposition and discussion of the main contributions. The papers are grouped according to the type of tax system they have dealt with: linear, piecewise linear and non-linear taxation.

Keywords: time use, labour supply, household production, child care, leisure, consumption

JEL codes: D13, D15, H21, H22, H24, J13, J16, J18

ISBNs: 9781009479325 (HB), 9781108972673 (PB), 9781108973007 (OC)
ISSNs: 2516-2276 (online), 2516-2268 (print)

Contents

1 Introduction

We define a family as a household consisting of two adults with at least one child. When there are no children we refer to the household as a couple. Households with only one individual we call singles. We think it fair to say that most of theoretical tax policy analysis takes singles as the basic behavioural unit, though often referring to 'the household' in general, and this reflects the historical roots of models of economic decisions in economic theory.

Despite the fact that the large majority of taxpayers live in couple or family households, family taxation occupies a rather peripheral place in the optimal income tax literature. It is usually viewed as dealing with specialised issues such as the design of transfer payments for families with young children, or the supposed impossibility of having a tax system with the three properties of: not distorting the decision on whether to get married; exhibiting marginal rate progressivity; and satisfying a condition for horizontal equity which claims that households with the same incomes should pay the same amount of tax. The first of these is very important, the second requires further discussion in countries in which cohabitation without marriage is becoming relatively common, and the third is simply a fallacy: horizontal equity does not require equal taxation of equal household incomes, because household income is an inaccurate measure of a household's standard of living.

In fact, we would argue, analysis of family taxation is of central importance to tax policy, concerning as it does the fundamentals of the design of the income tax system, and such issues as whether or not indirect taxation should be included in an optimal tax system, and if so how.

Occam's Razor is quite rightly a much-prized instrument in economic analysis: why complicate models with details that add nothing to the fundamental insights? This could be put forward as a rationalisation for ignoring the real nature of family households. Unfortunately this does not stand up against the arguments we will present here. Although there is absolutely no doubt that the body of theory developed for singles offers many insights and methods of analysis that are of great use in the theory of family taxation, there are important questions to which it gives no answers, or worse, implies misleading policy recommendations. One example of this is the proposition that indirect taxation, if it is used at all, should optimally be at a uniform rate. However the Atkinson and Stiglitz (1976) Theorem and more recent developments related to it show that this does not hold in general for family households.

There are two basic reasons for taking the family household as the behavioural unit for the economic analysis of taxation. The first was pointed out by

Paul Samuelson in his classic paper on social indifference curves.[1] Economic models give primacy to the well-being of individuals, and these are still the basic units of analysis, but many households consist of at least two individuals and so individual outcomes are mediated through joint decision taking. Households should best be thought of as social groups. Though they disagreed profoundly on details, both Samuelson and Gary Becker, usually regarded as the founder of modern family economics, agreed entirely on that point.

The second reason is the economic significance of household production, the use of household members' time and bought-in resources to provide goods and services for within-household consumption, such as child care, food preparation, financial planning, in-house entertainment, as well as all those necessary chores such as shopping, cleaning and doing laundry that perhaps many of us prefer not to think about. Time use studies show that household production is a very substantial, untaxed use of individuals' time and budget studies show that it involves a significant amount of their expenditure.[2] Gayle and Shephard (2019) provide an innovative analysis of optimal taxation by integrating a marriage market model with a collective household model in which individuals allocate their time between market work, household production and leisure activities.

The principle of Occam's Razor could suggest that this alone is not a reason for including household production explicitly in a model. Why not simply bundle household production with leisure time and stick with the formulation of individual utilities as functions of consumption and leisure, thus augmented? This has in fact been standard practice even in family economics. There are three main arguments against doing this, which we find convincing.

First is the considerable heterogeneity in second earner market labour supply. In recognition of the fact that in many countries there is still a significant degree of specialisation in household vs market work, we define the primary earner as the one who is more specialised in market work while the second earner does relatively more of the household production. It has become less accurate to define the two roles strictly in terms of gender, even if it may sometimes be convenient to do so. In the days when the traditional pattern of specialisation prevailed, where the husband went out to work and the wife stayed at home and did virtually all the household production, the labour supply decisions of the household relevant to tax analysis could reasonably be modelled as if it were a single individual. But since the 1950s and 1960s this pattern has been displaced by one in which the density function of hours worked by second earners on the

---

[1] Samuelson (1956).
[2] See also Browning and Gørtz (2012), Cherchye et al. (2012) and Lise and Yamada (2019).

interval from zero to full-time is not far off from uniform, with spikes at zero and full-time.[3]

Why should that matter? In a nutshell, because it implies that the joint labour earnings of a couple are no longer a reliable indicator of the level of well-being of the household members. This is determined in the aggregate by the sum of labour earnings and value of household production, just as the GDP of a country is determined by the value of its exports and domestically produced non-traded goods. Although it could be argued that this 'household GDP' is not the sole determinant of household well-being, just as in the case of countries, we would argue that it is a far better measure than household joint income.

This is one important reason for the claim that horizontal equity, if it is meant to apply to individual well-being no longer implies that households with the same joint market incomes are equally well off. At any given wage pair, market income and the time a second earner spends in household production are typically inversely related. Two couples with the same household income, one with a single-earner and the other with two earners, are unlikely to be equally well off. The latter household is very likely to have both lower consumption of household goods and less leisure time, and some of its expenditure has to be diverted to substitutes for home production. This must have an impact on the equity-efficiency trade-offs at the core of optimal tax analysis. The question of how the existence of significant levels of second earner labour supply and the income it generates should be taken account of in the tax system is an important one, and has strong implications for both across-household and within-household distributions of well-being.

Looked at from a somewhat different angle, if one individual in a couple has a close to zero income from market labour supply but a consumption level of market goods much higher than her earnings, then in a model without household production this must be regarded as resulting from an altruistic *transfer* from the primary earner, whereas in a model with household production, it can be seen as the outcome of the fundamental economic principle of *specialisation and exchange*. Such differences in perception should not be regarded as trivial. They are also relevant for tax analysis. Another, somewhat more sophisticated example of the potentially misleading effects of ignoring household production, discussed in Section 4, is the proposition that women's labour income should be taxed more heavily than men's because, if they have less bargaining power

---

[3] In some countries the roles of 'primary' and 'second' earners may have become a bit less closely identified with gender, but in the OECD countries on average it is still the case that around 80 per cent of second earners are female. For an interesting discussion see McClelland et al. (2014). Drawing on Australian data, Apps and Rees (2022) find a high degree of heterogeneity in second earner labour supply at a given primary wage.

in the household than the planner would like, then they are receiving too little leisure and therefore spending too much time in market work than is socially optimal. Being taxed out of the labour market is doing women a favour. This argument fails if the lack of bargaining power is reflected in having to specialise in household production and so supply less time to the market than the household might wish, an effect that is likely to be magnified by higher taxes on women as second earners.

The second reason for taking household production seriously is its implication for labour supply elasticities, a sufficient statistic central to optimal tax analysis. Why do women on average have much higher labour supply elasticities than men, whether at the intensive or the extensive margin? At the intensive margin, why would a second earner with the same wage as another and in a household with the same demographic characteristics supply far fewer hours in the labour market? In a model without household production, the usual answer is leisure preferences, since labour supply is determined by the marginal rate of substitution between leisure and consumption or income. Then a similar issue arises as in the case of singles: why should a household with higher labour income make a transfer to one with a lower income if the reason for the difference results simply from a stronger preference for leisure?

In a model with household production, on the other hand, the higher elasticity of market labour supply is simply explained by the fact that the second earner has a margin of substitution between work in the household and work in the market that exerts a stronger influence on labour supply choices for her than for the primary earner. Moreover, a difference in market labour supply between second earners in different households can be explained in terms of the feasible set: the households' elasticities of substitution between the second earner's time and bought-in inputs may differ because of differences in productivities, and/or there may be differences in prices and quality of bought-in inputs such as child care, differences in the wage rate of the primary earner and associated differences in demand for household goods. Welfare comparisons based on differences in market labour supplies between households arising from differences in feasible sets do not raise the same conceptual issues as differences due to preferences.

At the extensive margin, the usual explanation for non-participation in the labour market is the (assumed) fixed cost of work, for example commuting costs, the cost of work clothing, and so on. Sometimes foregone household production is also suggested, but it is a mistake to consider this only as a fixed cost. For example, with children in the household of an age at which they still require care, each hour the second earner spends in market work must be replaced by an hour's child care, and if that has to be bought in then the cost acts more like a tax per unit of labour supply than a fixed cost. Moreover, the costs associated with substituting bought-in market inputs for parental time can vary substantially across households, as exemplified again by child care: the hourly cost may vary from the opportunity cost of the time of a grandparent or other family member, through fees for child-minders or child-care centres, to the services of a posh nanny, with associated variations also in child care quality. Such quality-adjusted costs, and their variation across households, should not be ignored in the analysis of family taxation.

A more fruitful approach to the extensive margin question is not, we would argue, to regard it as a discrete choice between work or leisure, but rather as an allocation of non-leisure time between two types of work, in the household and in the labour market. An insight that results from this approach is that, if the household optimum is at a corner solution in its time allocation problem, the market wage that may be estimated for a (potential) second earner with a zero market labour supply is only a lower bound to her marginal value product in household production.

Finally, a third reason for taking household production seriously relates to the methodology of optimal tax analysis itself. Given the way this methodology has developed over the past four or five decades, there is something of a stumbling block created by the fact that the household has multiple dimensions of private information. There is not just the one dimension emphasised by James Mirrlees (1971) – innate ability as possibly reflected in the (unobservable) wage rate – though restricting attention simply to this already implies that a couple household must then have at least two dimensions of private information, which, as we show in Section 4, is a challenge to modelling the tax system. As we argue in greater detail in Section 3, the mechanism design approach is faced with a multidimensional screening problem the solutions of which are complex, not very robust to reasonable variations in assumptions, and not obviously applicable to real tax structures. Our conclusion from that, developed in Section 3, is that piecewise linear income taxation systems of the kind universally existing in reality should be at the forefront of the analysis.

The aim of all tax systems is to shift resources out of the ownership of private individuals so that they can be allocated to meet the purposes of government. In a monetary economy this is best done by monetary means, and so setting labour incomes as the tax base is an obvious place to start, even if that leaves a lot more to be said about the full set of possible tax instruments. In analysing how the income of family households should be taxed there are two basic modelling choices to be made: the choice of the behavioural model which specifies how the household responds to taxes and the choice of the income tax system.

Here, we survey the theoretical work published over the period from the mid-1980s to the mid-2010s that has applied the main forms of optimal income tax analysis – optimal linear, piecewise linear and non-linear taxation – to family taxation. In the course of doing that we discuss the household models that have mainly been used as the basis for the analysis of the behavioural responses to taxation.

2 Linear Income Taxation

We denote the adult individuals in a given household by $i = 1, 2$, the primary and second earners respectively,[4] and the households themselves by $h \in \mathcal{H} \subset \mathbb{R}_{++}$. The tax base consists of the incomes of the wage earners in the households, $y_{ih} = w_{ih}L_{ih}$, where L_{ih} is labour supply and w_{ih} the pretax wage rate. In defining primary and second earners we assume that $w_{1h} \geq w_{2h}$ and $L_{1h} \geq L_{2h}$, implying $y_{1h} \geq y_{2h}$. Wage rates are strictly positive and are defined on closed intervals $[w_{ih}^{\min}, w_{ih}^{\max}] \subset \mathbb{R}_{++}$, $i = 1, 2, h \in \mathcal{H}$. In models that ignore household production,[5] a *household type* is usually defined by its wage pair (w_{1h}, w_{2h}). There is at each w_{1h} a distribution of second earner wage rates conditional on w_{1h} with support $[w_{2h}^{\min}, w_{1h}]$.

Under a system of *linear joint taxation*, we represent the household's tax function as:

$$T(y_{1h}, y_{2h}) = -a + t(y_{1h} + y_{2h}) \tag{1}$$

where $a > 0$, often called the 'demogrant', is a lump sum transfer to the household and $t \in (0, 1)$ is the marginal tax rate (MTR). Three obvious properties of linear joint taxation are: first, that the MTRs facing individuals in the household are equalised; second, that the household's tax burden is strictly increasing in the tax rate and its joint income; and third, that the total tax paid is the same for all households with the same joint income, regardless of the composition of this sum as between the individual incomes, as well as of any other of the household's characteristics. Note that in tax systems where the tax rate increases with joint income, there is a fourth key property of joint taxation: the tax rate paid by one individual may increase with the income of the other, to an extent dependant on the size of the income difference and the degree of progressivity of the tax rates. This is often referred to as the *positive jointness* property.

---

[4] In this section we introduce the notation that will be used consistently for the discussion of all the work on which we report.

[5] This will be the case in the majority of models we discuss. Introduction of household production results in additional type variables, such as productivity in household work and cost of bought-in child care.

We take as the alternative to joint taxation the case of *individual taxation*, where the tax base is individual incomes and the tax rates on primary and second earners are allowed to differ. In that case the household's tax function is:

$$T(y_{1h}, y_{2h}) = -a + t_1 y_{1h} + t_2 y_{2h} \tag{2}$$

with $t_1 \gtreqqless t_2$. The two key properties therefore are that the tax rate of one earner is not directly affected by variations in the tax rate of the other, and that a household may have the same or higher joint income than another but be paying less tax, depending on the tax rates and the composition of the household's income as between the earnings of the two individuals. A further very important property in tax systems in which the tax rates increase with income is that the tax rate of one individual is unaffected by a change in the income of the other – there is *zero jointness*.

In the early 1970s a debate began in the USA around the question of whether the prevailing system of joint taxation should be replaced by an individual tax system. The main argument of the economists[6] in favour of the latter was that the labour supply elasticities for women were much higher than for men and so standard efficiency considerations based on the Ramsey Rule would suggest that women should be taxed at lower rates.

Proponents of joint taxation have on the other hand put forward essentially three arguments. The earliest[7] asserted that household members share their incomes equally, and therefore the commonly used form of joint taxation known as income splitting, under which the tax base is $(y_{1h} + y_{2h})/2$, puts each member of a two-earner household on the same footing as singles with the same income taxed at the same rate. A problem for this view is however that what evidence there is on the allocation of household income to the individual consumption expenditures of its members[8] suggests that a large proportion of total expenditure, around 60–70 per cent, is reported as 'for the household'. It is tempting to regard this as funding 'household public goods', but this does not correctly characterise a lot of this expenditure since the goods concerned, for example food, drink and tobacco, are both rival and excludable. Even if they were public goods in the strict sense, that would still not imply that the household members derive equal well-being from them. The proportions of

---

[6] See for example Boskin and Sheshinski (1983) and Rosen (1976).

[7] See for example Pechman (1977).

[8] See Browning and Gørtz (2012), Cherchye et al. (2012) and Lise and Yamada (2019) for data from Denmark, The Netherlands and Japan respectively. Also, Lise and Seitz (2011) show that UK data rejects the hypothesis that household consumption is allocated equally.

the shares in the remaining assignable expenditure going to individual earners, even if they do have a mean close to 50 per cent,[9] has a very large variance across households.

The second argument is based on the issue of horizontal equity among households (already alluded to in the Introduction). Suppose there is a linear joint income tax system. Household A has two earners working full time and earning $48,000 and $42,000 respectively, household B has only the primary earner in the labour market earning $48,000. If it is assumed that income is shared equally within households and that labour market income is taken as the measure of individual well-being, then the two individuals in A are much better off and therefore should, and in joint taxation systems do, pay more tax. But this is assuming that the second earner in B is making no contribution to household well-being. If however she is engaged in household production she could be producing (untaxed) goods and services, for example child care, which could be at least as valuable to the household as the labour market income earned by the second earner in A. At root, the income splitting argument is ignoring the issues raised by the wide variance in second earner labour supply across households and the significance of household production.

The main general message from the example is that joint labour income is an unreliable index of well-being primarily because across the equilibrium allocations of the population of households, individual well-being and household income may not necessarily show a monotonically increasing relationship.[10] If we change the example to the case in which the primary earner in household B earns $90,000 a year it is very hard, for the same reason as before, to believe that the households are equally well off. It also suggests that we need to find an explanation of across-household heterogeneity of second earner labour supply that is relevant to the analysis of optimal income taxation.

The third argument is equally problematic, and is directed at a supposed advantage of joint over individual taxation in terms of within-household economic efficiency. To discuss this we need a model of the household, so we take the simplest possible one, the so-called 'unitary model'. Define the household utility maximisation problem as:

$$\max_{x_h, l_{ih}, L_{ih}} U(x_h, L_{1h}, L_{2h}) \text{ s.t. } x_h = \sum_{i=1,2} w_{ih} L_{ih} \tag{3}$$

---

[9] This is the case for Denmark and the Netherlands, but in Japan the shares of expenditure on assignable goods is very far from equal.

[10] This argument is well understood by many economists and yet the tax systems in major economies like France, Germany, Japan and the US, though they have important differences, are still based on income splitting.

$U(.)$ has all the properties of a standard *individual* utility function, it treats the household as an individual with two forms of labour supply. The price of the numéraire composite consumption good x is normalised to 1 so wages are in units of consumption. Then under linear joint taxation the first order conditions (FOC) for this problem, assuming an interior solution with both $L_{ih} > 0$, yield the condition:

$$\frac{\partial U(L_{1h})}{\partial U(L_{2h})} = \frac{(1-t)w_{1h}}{(1-t)w_{2h}} = \frac{w_{1h}}{w_{2h}} \tag{4}$$

whereas under gender-based taxation[11] with rates t_1, t_2 we would have

$$\frac{\partial U(L_{1h})}{\partial U(L_{2h})} = \frac{(1-t_1)w_{1h}}{(1-t_2)w_{2h}} \tag{5}$$

which, if $t_1 \neq t_2$, implies that the choice of labour supplies in the household does not satisfy the condition for Pareto efficiency, whereas under joint taxation it does. Thus at any tax revenue requirement joint taxation must imply a smaller deadweight welfare loss. The problem with this argument is that it ignores the well-known Theorem of the Second Best, which tells us that in an economy with an irremovable Pareto inefficient distortion in one sector, in this case in the labour market, it will in general be second best optimal to have compensating distortions in related sectors, in this case the within household labour supply allocations. To find out what really is optimal we have to carry out the optimal tax analysis, allowing tax rates to differ.

Boskin and Sheshinski (1983) were the first to apply the formal optimal taxation methodology to the issue of family taxation. Their starting point was the intuition suggested by the Ramsey condition, as just noted. They first show in a representative household model that the Ramsey proposition holds under a specific, quite plausible assumption: if the compensated cross elasticities between the primary and second earners' labour supplies are sufficiently small relative to their own compensated elasticities that they can be set to zero,[12] then the Ramsey result holds: second earners should have a lower tax rate because of their higher compensated own-elasticity.

However, as we know from the standard analysis[13] an optimal linear tax system depends on considerations of both efficiency and equity, and their formal optimal tax analysis, which extends optimal linear tax theory to the case of

---

[11] Or, more precisely, individual taxation, where the tax base is individual income and the tax rates on primary and second earners respectively are allowed to differ.

[12] Empirical evidence suggests that changes in women's wages do not have a significant effect on male labour supplies, while the converse is also true except possibly at the top end of the income distribution, where they are weakly negative.

[13] See Sheshinski (1972).

couple households, does not show conclusively that the undeniable efficiency gains in switching from a joint to an individual tax system necessarily outweigh the possibility that on equity grounds it may be optimal to have a higher tax on female labour supply. As Apps and Rees (1999) show, in a tax reform analysis with a revenue-neutral switch from joint to individual taxation, if the marginal tax rate on second earners falls while that on primary earners rises, households with a high second earner labour supply gain and those with a low-to-zero second earner labour supply may lose. This follows because in a model without household production, as in Boskin and Sheshinski, in equilibrium household utilities across households increase monotonically with joint income, and so single earner households will tend to be among the worst off and therefore may have relatively high social welfare weights. Boskin and Sheshinski's analysis in fact has the general result that second earner tax rates could optimally be higher or lower than those on primary earners, which at least implies that the case in which tax rates are equalised, that is joint taxation, is a very special case. Their conclusion that the tax rate on second earners should be lower than that on primary earners is based on a numerical version of their model which has standard assumptions on utility and labour supply functions and is calibrated on the then available data. We now discuss these results a little more formally.

Note first that the solution of the problem in (3) with $t_1 \gtreqless t_2$ yields the standard indirect household utility functions $V_h(a, t_1, t_2)$. Given a joint density function $\phi(w_1, w_2)$, strictly positive everywhere on $\mathcal{H}$, the optimal tax problem becomes:

$$\max_{a, t_1, t_2} \mathcal{S} = \int \int_{\mathcal{H}} S(V_h(a, t_1, t_2)) \phi(w_1, w_2) dw_1 dw_2 \tag{6}$$

subject to:

$$\int \int_{\mathcal{H}} \sum_i t_i w_i L_i(a, t_1, t_2) \phi(w_1, w_2) dw_1 dw_2 - a \geq R \tag{7}$$

where $R \gtreqless 0$ is a per capita revenue requirement.

Although the Boskin/Sheshinski paper gives the first order conditions for this problem, such is the level of generality that these do not as they stand add any real insights. They certainly do not at this level of generality allow a proof that an optimum implies $t_2 < t_1$. Boskin/Sheshinski therefore make the assumption of perfect assortative matching, with $w_2 = \psi(w_1)$ and $\psi(.)$ strictly increasing and differentiable. In that case they can reduce the problem to one dimension, with $w_1 \in [w_1^{\min}, w_1^{\max}]$, and rewrite it as

$$\max_{a,t_i} \mathcal{S} = \int_{w_1^{\min}}^{w_1^{\max}} S(V_h(a,t_1,t_2))dF_1 \text{ s.t.} \int_{w_1^{\min}}^{w_1^{\max}} \sum_i t_i w_i L_i dF_1 - a - R \geq 0 \quad (8)$$

where $F_1(w_1)$ is the distribution function for w_1 with support $[w_1^{\min}, w_1^{\max}]$.

The first order conditions of this problem yield, after replacing the uncompensated derivatives with the corresponding Slutsky equations and rearranging terms:

$$t_i = \frac{\int_{w_1^{\min}}^{w_1^{\max}} [(\mu(w_1) - 1)y_i]dF_1}{\int_{w_1^{\min}}^{w_1^{\max}} y_i \eta_i dF_1} \quad i = 1,2 \quad (9)$$

where $\mu(w_1)$ is the marginal social utility of income of household $h=(w_1, \psi(w_1))$ with a mean value of 1, the $\eta_i < 0$ are the compensated elasticities of labour supply with respect to the tax rate and the numerator is the covariance of the household's net marginal social utility of income with income, which on Boskin/Sheshinski's assumptions is also negative. Although, *other things being equal*, the ratio t_1/t_2 will be higher the larger the ratio η_2/η_1 across the wage distribution, we still have some work to do to understand why we should have $t_1 > t_2$. Note that for $t_1 = t_2$ the higher absolute value of the deadweight loss term has to be exactly offset by a higher absolute value of the covariance of the marginal social utility of the household income with individual income, so joint taxation is strictly optimal only in a knife-edge case.

In the literature on optimal linear income taxation it is usual to regard the expression in the denominator as a measure of the efficiency effect of the tax, while the numerator can be viewed as measuring the distributional effect. The optimal tax trades off the marginal redistributive power of the tax against its marginal efficiency cost. If the tax on women's income is both less powerful as a redistributive instrument and more costly, that would pretty well clinch the Boskin/Sheshinski argument. Given their assumption of perfect assortative matching, and the fact that the gender wage gap widens as we move up through the income distribution, we can construct a simple argument that shows just that.

For simplicity, suppose that $y_2 = ky_1$, $k \in (0,1)$. Then we can write:

$$t_2 = \frac{\int_{w_1^{\min}}^{w_1^{\max}} [(\mu(w_1) - 1)ky_1]dF_1}{\int_{w_1^{\min}}^{w_1^{\max}} ky_1 \eta_2 dF_1} = \frac{\int_{w_1^{\min}}^{w_1^{\max}} [(\mu(w_1) - 1)y_1]dF_1}{\int_{w_1^{\min}}^{w_1^{\max}} y_1 \eta_2 dF_1} < t_1 \quad (10)$$

With $|\eta_2| > |\eta_1|$ across all households the inequality must then hold. Intuitively, with perfect assortative matching the tax rate t_2 cannot be a sufficiently more powerful instrument of redistribution across households than t_1 to offset the higher deadweight loss associated with the latter.

We cannot really say more at this point than that the Boskin/Sheshinski analysis, given its assumptions, supports the conjecture that individual taxation is welfare superior to joint taxation, but further work is necessary. In particular, we need to test the robustness of that conclusion by considering tax systems that have structures closer to those of real tax systems. This is the subject of the next section.

3 Piecewise Linear Income Taxation

In most of the countries in the world that have income tax systems, the formal structure of these is piecewise linear. That is, the income tax base is partitioned into tax brackets within each of which there is a given, constant tax rate,[14] and these usually increase as we move upward through the income distribution (marginal rate progressivity). An individual's marginal tax rate is that of the highest bracket their income reaches. Income in the lower, intramarginal brackets is taxed at the rates corresponding to those brackets. The main reason for extending the analysis of linear taxation is that, as well as its being more relevant for real-world tax systems, we can now take into account the issue of marginal rate progressivity and the structure of the tax system more generally.

This fairly simple structure is however usually complicated by what are effectively income taxes or subsidies from other parts of the public finance system. For example, in some countries such as the US and UK low wage workers receive supplements to their earned income. More generally, families with children may receive child benefits that are withdrawn as a function of some income measure above a certain level, and social insurance contributions and/or benefits may be related to income and so are in effect part of the income tax system. The complexities in the system are usually caused by the wish to 'tag' certain groups of households with readily identifiable characteristics, but this still leaves large groups of people, with varying abilities to earn income, facing the same marginal tax rates.[15] In the rest of this section, we work with a fairly simple two-bracket piecewise linear system. Here, we continue to focus on the issue of joint *vs.* individual tax bases.

From the point of view of optimal tax analysis, the essential property of all these systems, however complicated, is that they induce a *pooling equilibrium* on the set of household types: households with different characteristics that

---

[14] The most notable exception to this is Germany, where in two middle tax brackets the marginal tax rate increases linearly with income. This makes the primary earner's tax rate particularly sensitive to the second earner's labour supply decision over the relevant income brackets, creating very strong positive jointness.

[15] We will return to this point in the next section, where we discuss optimal non-linear taxation.

are relevant to their tax treatment, but whose income puts them in the same marginal tax bracket, face the same rate. This is in sharp contrast to the non-linear tax systems studied in the next section, where an essential part of the model structure is a set of incentive compatibility constraints designed to ensure a *separating equilibrium* of types – each type has in general its own marginal tax rate and lump sum. This creates important differences both in the interpretation and in the empirical applicability of the two types of model. It can be shown that a non-linear tax system is welfare superior to a linear tax system over a given population of wage earners,[16] but the empirical significance of this difference is unclear in the case of a piecewise linear system with a sufficiently large number of brackets.[17]

As well as the issue of the choice of tax base as between joint and individual incomes, also central is the structure of the rate scale, in particular whether the marginal tax rates applying to successive income brackets should be strictly increasing, or whether over at least some income ranges they should be decreasing. We refer to these as the convex and nonconvex cases respectively, to describe the types of budget sets in the gross income-net income/consumption plane to which they give rise. For the purposes of this Element, we focus on the convex case of a two-bracket piecewise linear system.[18]

By individual taxation we now mean the case in which the individual earners' incomes are taxed separately but according to the same tax schedule. This differs therefore from tax systems with rate structures that differentiate between primary and second earners, which we term here 'selective'. The main reason for constraining the rate schedules to be identical under individual taxation is that in practice, piecewise linear tax systems that are not joint are in fact overwhelmingly of this kind. Moreover, if individual taxation yields higher social welfare than joint taxation under realistic assumptions, this result applies *a fortiori* to selective taxation, since removing the constraint that tax schedules must be identical cannot reduce the maximised value of social welfare and would be expected to increase it.[19]

The approach we adopt is the standard one of characterising the sufficient statistics that determine in general terms the optimal values of the instruments

---

[16] See Boadway (1988).

[17] See Andrienko et al. (2016).

[18] Apps et al. (2014) show that for wage distributions such as those currently prevailing in many OECD countries convex systems are highly likely to be welfare optimal. This is in contrast to Slemrod et al. (1994), which, using a log-normal wage distribution based on data from the early 1970s, obtained the result that the optimal two-bracket piecewise linear tax system was nonconvex.

[19] It is quite straightforward to extend the analysis to two different piecewise linear tax systems for primary and second earners.

in the taxation system.[20] These are the marginal social utilities of income and the derivatives of labour supplies or incomes with respect to the tax instruments at the optimal tax system. This allows us to make qualitative statements about the differences between the two systems. To do this, all we need to know about the households' preferences are their indirect utility functions defined on the variables defining the instruments of tax system, which we denote by $V_h(.)$, and a social welfare function of the usual kind. However, it also has to be kept in mind that underlying these derivatives and determining their values, implicitly or, preferably, explicitly, is a behavioural model of the household. In particular, any attempt to provide empirical estimates of the sufficient statistics for a discussion of actual tax policy must be based on such a model, and the one selected will have a crucial impact on the results. We consider this point further after we have set out the optimal tax analysis in the following two subsections.

3.1 Joint Taxation

There is a two-bracket piecewise linear tax[21] on total household labour earnings, defined by the vector $(\alpha, \tau_1, \tau_2, \eta)$, where α is the uniform lump sum paid to every household, τ_1, τ_2 are the marginal tax rates in the lower and upper brackets of the tax schedule, and η is the value of *joint earnings* defining the bracket limit. The household tax function is $T(y_{1h}, y_{2h}) \equiv T(y_h)$, with $y_h = \sum_{i=1}^{2} y_{ih}$. This tax function is given by:

$$T(y_h) = -\alpha + \tau_1 y_h \quad y_h \leq \eta \tag{11}$$

$$T(y_h) = -\alpha + \tau_2 y_h + (\tau_1 - \tau_2)\eta \quad y_h > \eta \tag{12}$$

Given that all households face this identical budget constraint, the optimal income y_h^* for any one household must be in one of three possible subsets, which give a partition $\{\mathcal{H}_0, \mathcal{H}_1, \mathcal{H}_2\}$ of the set $\mathcal{H}$ defined as follows:

$$\mathcal{H}_0 = \{\, h \mid 0 \leq y_h^* < \eta \} \tag{13}$$

$$\mathcal{H}_1 = \{\, h \mid y_h^* = \eta \} \tag{14}$$

$$\mathcal{H}_2 = \{\, h \mid y_h^* > \eta \} \tag{15}$$

A household's optimum income may be either in the lower tax bracket, or at the kink in the budget constraint defined by the bracket limit η, or in the upper tax bracket. The assumption of a continuum of households and continuity of utility functions implies that there is necessarily 'bunching' at the kink, in the sense

---

[20] See Chetty (2009).

[21] For an extension of optimum piecewise linear taxation to the case of an arbitrary number $m \geq 2$ of tax brackets see Andrienko et al. (2016).

that a non-empty subset of households is in the position whereby they would increase their labour supply at the tax rate t_1 but do not want to do so at the tax rate t_2. In all of what follows we assume that we are dealing with tax systems in which each of these subsets is non-empty. Total household gross and net income are increasing continuously as we move from $\mathcal{H}_0$ to $\mathcal{H}_1$ and from $\mathcal{H}_1$ to $\mathcal{H}_2$, while they are both constant in $\mathcal{H}_1$ (though of course individual incomes in these households may vary across households, as long as they sum to η).

3.1.1 Optimal Tax Analysis

We assume that the household utility functions are quasilinear (though essentially this just simplifies interpretation of the results). Given the household indirect utility functions $V_h(.)$, the planner solves

$$\max_{\alpha,\tau_1,\tau_2,\eta} W = \int_{h\in\mathcal{H}} S(V_h(\alpha,\tau_1,\tau_2,\eta))dF \tag{16}$$

subject to the public sector budget constraint

$$\tau_1\left[\int_{h\in\mathcal{H}_0} y_h dF + \eta\int_{h\in\mathcal{H}_1} dF\right] + \int_{h\in\mathcal{H}_2}[\tau_2 y_h + (\tau_1-\tau_2)\eta]dF \geq \alpha \tag{17}$$

where $S(.)$ is a strictly concave and increasing function expressing the planner's distributional preferences over household utilities. We assume the aim of taxation is purely redistributive. Of course, exactly which households will be in which subsets is determined at the optimum, and depends on the values of the tax parameters. The following discussion characterises the optimal solution *given* the allocation of households to subsets that obtains at this optimum.

From the first order conditions characterising the optimal tax variables we can derive the conditions:

$$\int_{\mathcal{H}}(\sigma_h - 1)dF = 0 \tag{18}$$

$$\tau_1^* = \frac{\int_{\mathcal{H}_0}(\sigma_h - 1)y_h^* dF + \eta^*\int_{\mathcal{H}_1\cup\mathcal{H}_2}(\sigma_h - 1)dF}{\int_{\mathcal{H}_0}(\partial y_h/\partial\tau_1)dF} \tag{19}$$

$$\tau_2^* = \frac{\int_{\mathcal{H}_2}(\sigma_h - 1)(y_h^* - \eta^*)dF}{\int_{\mathcal{H}_2}(\partial y_h/\partial\tau_2)dF} \tag{20}$$

$$\int_{\mathcal{H}_1}\left\{\sigma_h\left[(1-\tau_1) - \frac{\partial\psi}{\partial y_h}\right] + \tau_1^*\right\}dF = -(\tau_2^* - \tau_1^*)\int_{\mathcal{H}_2}(\sigma_h - 1)dF \tag{21}$$

Condition (18) follows from the quasilinearity of the utility functions and is familiar from linear tax theory: with λ the shadow price of the government budget constraint, $\sigma_h \equiv S'(v_h)/\lambda$ is the marginal social utility of income to household h in terms of the numeraire, consumption, and so the optimal lump sum α equalises the average of the marginal social utilities of household income across the population to the marginal cost of the lump sum, which is 1. The value of the deviation from the average $(\sigma_h - 1) \gtreqless 0$ is the *distributional characteristic* of household h.

The strict concavity of $S(.)$ implies that σ_h is strictly decreasing in v_h. In the standard income tax model, with V_h and y_h co-monotonic, the lower tax bracket would contain not only the lower incomes but also the lower utilities. But if the household model does not imply this co-monotonicity, the lower tax bracket may contain households with higher utility than households that are assigned, on the basis of joint income, to the higher bracket. The tax system assigns households to tax brackets on the basis of income, not utility, and redistributes accordingly.

In the two conditions corresponding to the tax rates τ_1^*, τ_2^*, the denominators are the frequency-weighted sums of the compensated derivatives of joint earnings with respect to the tax rates over the relevant subsets, and so are negative and give a measure of the marginal deadweight loss of the tax rate at the optimum, the efficiency cost of the tax, for households in the indicated subsets. The numerators give the equity effects.

The two terms in the numerator of (19) correspond to the two ways in which the lower bracket tax rate affects the contributions households make to funding the lump sum payment α. It is the interaction of these two terms which can lead to the nonconvex case in which the upper bracket tax rate is optimally lower than that in the lower bracket, as in Slemrod et al. (1994).[22]

Given their optimal household earnings y_h^*, the first term gives the sum of the effects of a marginal tax rate change on utility, weighted by the distributional characteristic, over subset $\mathcal{H}_0$. The second term reflects the fact that the lower bracket tax rate is effectively a lump sum tax on income earned by the two higher income brackets, $\mathcal{H}_1$ and $\mathcal{H}_2$, since a change in this tax rate has only an intramarginal effect, changing the tax they pay at a rate η, while leaving their (compensated) labour supply unchanged.

Although the interpretation of the results owes more to the theory of linear taxation than that of nonliner taxation (see Section 4) in this respect the two theories are similar. This is not to claim that if we were to let the bracket width go to zero we would obtain the optimal non-linear function since here we have no incentive compatibility constraint. On the other hand, faced with this tax system the households do 'honestly' reveal their types.

Only the first of these two effects is present in the condition (20) corresponding to the higher tax rate, simply because there is no higher tax bracket. The

---

[22] For further discussion see Apps et al. (2014).

portion of the income of a household in the higher tax bracket that is taxed at the rate τ_2^* is $(y_h^* - \eta^*)$, and this is weighted by its distributional characteristic. Note that, unlike the case of linear income taxation, these numerator terms are not covariances, since the mean of σ_h over each of the subsets is not 1. We can still interpret them however as expressing the power of the tax instrument to redistribute utility by redistributing income within the bracket concerned.

Note also that, other things equal, the more sharply y_h^* increases across households in the upper bracket the greater will be the tax rate τ_2^*, implying that tax rates are sensitive to growing inequality in the form of sharp increases in top incomes.[23]

Condition (21), corresponding to the optimal bracket limit η^*, has the following interpretation. The left-hand side represents the marginal social benefit of a relaxation of the bracket limit. This consists first of the gain to all those households that are effectively constrained at η^*, in the sense that they are prepared to increase earnings if these are taxed at τ_1^* but not at τ_2^*: the return to additional labour supply at τ_1^*, but not τ_2^*, exceeds its marginal utility cost. The first term in brackets on the left hand side is the net marginal benefit to these consumers, weighted by their distributional characteristics. The second term is the rate at which tax revenue increases given the increase in gross income resulting from the relaxation of the bracket limit.

The right hand side gives the marginal social cost of the relaxation. Since $(\tau_2^* - \tau_1^*) > 0$ by assumption, all households $h \in \mathcal{H}_2$ receive a lump sum income increase at this rate and this is weighted by the distributional characteristic of these households. As long as the sum of these deviations, weighted by the densities of the household types, is negative, the marginal cost of the bracket limit increase is a worsening in the equity of the income distribution. The condition then trades off the marginal social value of the gain to households in $\mathcal{H}_1$ against the marginal social cost of making households in $\mathcal{H}_2$ better off. Of course, an important but unspecified determinant of these results is the density function of household types. Just as in the Boskin/Sheshinski model, this restricts the conclusions we can draw in general and makes empirical work on these models essential.

3.2 Individual Taxation

Under individual taxation there is a two-bracket piecewise linear tax system now applied to individual labour earnings, defined by the vector (a, t_1, t_2, y), where a is again a uniform lump sum paid to every household, (it would also

---

[23] See Andrienko et al. (2016) for more on this.

be of interest to assume that demogrants could be paid separately to each individual in the household), t_1, t_2 are the marginal tax rates in the lower and upper brackets respectively, and y is the value of *individual earnings* defining the bracket. Thus the individual tax function $\hat{T}(y_{ih})$ is defined by:

$$\hat{T}(y_{ih}) = t_1 y_{ih} \quad y_{ih} \leq y \tag{22}$$

$$\hat{T}(y_{ih}) = t_2 y_{ih} + (t_1 - t_2)y \quad y_{ih} > y \quad h \in \mathcal{H} \tag{23}$$

and the household tax function is

$$T(y_{1h}, y_{2h}) = -a + \sum_{i=1}^{2} \hat{T}(y_{ih}). \tag{24}$$

Given that, by definition, $y_{2h}^* \leq y_{1h}^*$ for every household, and that under individual taxation everyone faces the same tax schedule, there are now six possible subsets of households which form a partition $\{H_0, H_1, ..., H_5\}$ of the index set $\mathcal{H}$, defined by

$$H_0 = \{\, h \mid 0 \leq y_{ih}^* < y, \ i = 1,2 \,\} \tag{25}$$

$$H_1 = \{\, h \mid y_{2h}^* < y = y_{1h}^* \,\} \tag{26}$$

$$H_2 = \{\, h \mid y_{ih}^* = y, \ i = 1,2 \,\} \tag{27}$$

$$H_3 = \{\, h \mid y_{2h}^* < y < y_{1h}^* \,\} \tag{28}$$

$$H_4 = \{\, h \mid y_{2h}^* = y < y_{1h}^* \,\} \tag{29}$$

$$H_5 = \{\, h \mid y_{ih}^* > y, \ i = 1,2 \,\} \tag{30}$$

In H_0, H_1, H_2 both individuals face the lower marginal tax rate, in H_3 and H_4 the primary earner alone faces the higher marginal tax rate while the second earner pays the lower tax rate, and in H_5 both face the higher rate.

From this, it is easy to see that increasing the number of tax brackets just increases the number of subsets that have to be defined, but nothing changes the underlying principle. For the extension to more than two tax brackets see Andrienko et al. (2016).

To shorten notation we denote the subset $H_i \cup H_j$ by H_{ij}, and $H_i \cup H_j \cup H_k$ by H_{ijk}, $i,j,k = 0,...,5$, $i \neq j$, $i,j \neq k$. The planner solves

$$\max_{a,t_1,t_2,y} W = \int_{\mathcal{H}} S(v_h)dF$$

subject now to the public sector budget constraint

$$\int_{H_{012}} t_1 y_h dF + \int_{H_{34}} [t_2 y_{1h} + t_1 y_{2h} + (t_1 - t_2)y]dF + \int_{H_5} [t_2 y_h + 2(t_1 - t_2)y]dF \geq a \tag{31}$$

where again $y_h = \sum_{i=1}^{2} y_{ih}$.

In what follows it will be useful to denote by μ_{ih} the value of a relaxation of the bracket limit to an individual at the kink in the budget constraint. Also, to shorten notation we denote $\sigma_h - 1$ by δ_h. Then $\delta_h > (<)0$ according as household h is relatively worse (better) off *in utility terms* than the subset of households for which $\sigma_h = 1$.

From the first order conditions for an optimal solution we derive:

$$\int_{\mathcal{H}} \delta_h dF = 0 \tag{32}$$

$$t_1^* = \frac{\int_{H_0} \delta_h y_h^* dF + \int_{H_{13}} \delta_h (y_{2h}^* + y^*) dF + 2y^* \int_{H_{245}} \delta_h dF}{\int_{H_0} \partial y_{1h}/\partial t_1 dF + \int_{H_{013}} \partial y_{2h}/\partial t_1 dF} \tag{33}$$

$$t_2^* = \frac{\int_{H_{345}} \delta_h (y_{1h}^* - y^*) dF + \int_{H_5} \delta_h (y_{2h}^* - y^*) dF}{\int_{H_{345}} \partial y_{1h}/\partial t_2 dF + \int_{H_5} \partial y_{2h}/\partial t_2 dF} \tag{34}$$

$$\int_{H_{12}} (\sigma_h \mu_{1h} + t_1) dF + \int_{H_{24}} (\sigma_h \mu_{2h} + t_1) dF$$

$$= -(t_2 - t_1) \left[\int_{H_{34}} \delta_h dF + 2 \int_{H_5} \delta_h dF \right] \tag{35}$$

The first condition, since it involves the entire population, is exactly as for joint taxation, though of course the distribution of marginal social utilities will in general differ. The remaining three conditions have basically the same interpretation as before, but of course the relevant integrals are now over subsets of individuals reflecting the partition defined in (25)–(30).

To begin an analysis of the differences in social welfare under the two systems, we carry out the following thought experiment. We make the unrealistic assumptions that with joint taxation the bracket limit is η, while under individual taxation it is $\eta/2$, and also that marginal tax rates are the same in both cases. It is very unlikely to be true of the optimal individual tax system because of the effects on labour supply choices of a switch between systems. Nonetheless it is useful in clarifying some ideas.

We can think of any tax system as specifying a rule for assigning individuals and households to tax brackets, and the basic question we now address is: what are the implications of the respective assignment rules specified by the two systems here for the efficiency and equity of taxation?

First, consider only the difference in the *equity effects* of the two systems. On the given assumptions:

- Households in which both earners face the lower tax rate are equally well off under the two systems, they face the same tax rates as before.
- Under individual taxation, the primary earners in households where the higher earner only is in the higher bracket, in the subset of incomes

$y_{1h} = (\eta/2, \eta]$, now pay the higher tax rate while the second earners pay the lower tax rate just as before, so these households become worse off than under joint taxation. Essentially, the primary earners lose the advantage of income splitting.

- Under individual taxation, primary earners with incomes higher than η again pay the higher tax rate but second earners with incomes below pay the lower tax rate instead of the higher one, so these households may become better or worse off than under joint taxation, depending on their levels of second income. The higher the second income, the more likely it is that the household is better off.

- Under individual taxation, households where the higher income primary earners have incomes higher than η and therefore paid the higher tax rate under joint taxation, but whose second earners have incomes lower than $\eta/2$ so that they now pay the lower tax rate, become strictly better off.

- Finally, in households in which both earners still pay the higher tax rate, as they did under joint taxation, they are just as well off as before.

Clearly there are losers and gainers as we move between the two systems. The point to emphasise however is that the overall evaluation from the viewpoint of social welfare depends not only on the joint distribution function of income pairs but also on the role played by household production.

As mentioned earlier, if household well-being is monotonically increasing with household income then from the equity point of view some households that gain will have higher incomes than some households that lose when the primary earner loses the income splitting advantage. Thus, although, given the standard elasticity assumptions, there is an unambiguous reduction in deadweight losses, on equity grounds one might oppose the change. Suppose, on the other hand, that at *any given primary income* the inverse relationship between market income and the value of household production is such as to at least broadly equalise household GDP, the sum of household labour market earnings and the value of household production. Then, whereas the 'assignment rule' under joint taxation is to put households with higher joint market earnings into the higher tax bracket, the assignment rule under individual taxation is to put households with higher primary earner income into the higher bracket. If, then, we assume that the household GDP increases with primary income, we can view individual taxation as providing an implicit tax on the value of household production, and the equity effects of the switch to individual taxation are far less adverse.

Though it can give useful insights, this example does not allow us to make a full comparison of the differences between the two *optimal* tax systems since it excludes labour supply effects. We can take the interpretation further however with a pairwise comparison of each of the optimality conditions (19)–(21) and (33)–(35) in the two tax systems from the point of view of their efficiency effects.

The numerators of the conditions for the marginal tax rates τ_1^* and t_1^* have the same general structure, with one component based on the incomes of individuals in the lower tax bracket weighted by the distributional terms, the other reflecting the lump sum tax effects on individuals at the kink and in the higher brackets, similarly weighted by distributional terms. The numerators in the conditions for τ_2^* and t_2^* do not contain the second component. However, the similarities end there. The compositions of the subsets over which the weighted sums are taken will be very different. First note that the denominator in the expression for t_1^* will tend to contain more lower income second earners, since the subset H_{013} contains second earners who, because they are in households with high wage primary earners, would under joint taxation be in the upper tax bracket. The subset H_{345} in the denominator for t_2^* will tend to include more high wage primary earners, who have lost the income-splitting advantage they obtain under joint taxation. Other things equal therefore, this would lead us to expect a greater difference between the two tax rates, or higher marginal rate progressivity, in the case of individual taxation, given the stylised fact that labour supply elasticities are lower for primary than for second earners.

We should note that the empirical estimates of elasticities are gender-based – female labour supply elasticities are higher than male – whereas the distinction here between primary and second earners is on the basis of earned income rather than gender. We would argue however that the high female elasticities are based on role rather than gender. Also, as pointed out earlier, it is still the case that the large majority of second earners are women. For insightful empirical work on this, see McClelland et al. (2014).

The approach to the tax analysis based on the sufficient statistics methodology is useful in allowing the characteristics of the optimal tax system to be derived in a general sense, but cannot itself tell us which would be better in terms of the value of some specified Social Welfare Function. For this we would also have to specify the model of household behaviour that underlies the tax analysis. Moreover, since qualitative differences might be very difficult to identify, we would need to parametrise this model and estimate values of the numerical differences in the outcomes of the two systems.

Apps and Rees (2018) do this by setting up a model and calibrating it with Australian labour market data. An important feature of the individual utility functions in the household model is that they depend not only on the consumption of a market good and leisure, but also on household production in the form of child care. Moreover, the parameters determining the implicit prices of the household good may vary across households. In particular, productivities in household production increase with household wage rates, reflecting the effects both of parental human capital and higher household income.

The results of the model simulations show that individual taxation welfare-dominates joint taxation over a wide range of empirically reasonable parameter values. This is due not only to the efficiency gain from individual taxation; there is also a gain in the equity of the welfare distribution. An important reason for this is the high degree of inequality at the top of the empirical primary earner wage distribution, which allows high income primary earners to benefit substantially from income splitting in a joint taxation system. Taking account of household production also helps to correct the bias, in the welfare ranking that is created by a tax system based on joint income, against lower wage households with both earners working full time.

4 Optimal Non-linear Taxation of Couples

In the theory of optimal non-linear income taxation developed for singles, inaugurated by James Mirrlees (1971), there is a given set of individual workers/consumers who differ along a single dimension, their innate 'ability' or more concretely productivity in market work, which is often identified with their wage. If planners could identify the innate ability type of each worker they could use purely lump sum taxation to achieve the desired redistribution without distorting labour supplies at the margin: the conditions for Pareto efficiency remain satisfied, the economy moves costlessly around its aggregate utility frontier. However, when productivity type is not verifiably observable, they have to resort to distortionary income taxation, which moves the economy inside its utility frontier. The theory then seeks to explore the trade-off between the benefit from taxation, often assumed to be purely in the form of income redistribution, and the cost, in terms of the deadweight loss from tax distortions, the 'limit to redistribution', that results.

It is often pointed out that an *optimal* income tax should not, as is the case in optimal linear taxation, constrain the set of possible solutions by specifying a priori a fixed structure for the optimal tax functions. An optimal tax should determine this structure endogenously as an outcome of the analysis. Though it is difficult to dispute the logic of this approach, this results, as we shall see, in a significant loss in tractability of the analysis and is prone to produce results that bear little resemblance to real tax systems. This in itself may be no bad thing but it can make it difficult to relate the results to real-world policy debates. One also needs to be confident that the underlying behavioural model does successfully take into account all the key aspects of the real situation. Considerations of tractability tend to obscure this point.

Given the assumption of information asymmetry that characterises the non-linear approach, the Revelation Principle tells us that, under the assumptions of the model, the planner can do nothing better than to offer a menu of tax pairs consisting of a lump sum tax or subsidy and a marginal tax rate. This menu is constructed in such a way that the pair designed for each ability (wage) type will actually be selected by that type. An alternative but equivalent description of the process is to say that individuals declare an income to the planner who then gives them a tax pair, and an incentive-compatible system is one which induces them to report the income that corresponds under the tax system to their true type. Hence the constraints are sometimes called 'truth-telling' constraints and deviating from that is often referred to as 'mimicking' a different type. That is, the optimal tax structure is determined as a separating equilibrium solution to a mechanism design problem. This leads to a relatively tractable set of analytical procedures for deriving and characterising the optimal tax system: Find, within the set of tax systems that satisfy this 'self-selection' or 'incentive compatibility' (*IC*) condition, that system which maximises the social welfare function subject to the government budget constraint. This constraint plays the role of the participation constraint in standard principal/agent problems, though of course in the case of the tax system participation is mandatory. An additional *IC* constraint then creates a second-best tax problem. Boadway (1988) shows in this setting that solving this problem gives a higher social welfare level than an optimal linear tax.

If we now recognise that households consist of two earners, the extension of this approach seems rather obvious. We simply add a second wage-earner to the household. Her innate productivity is likewise private information. We then proceed with the analysis just as before.[24] In the language of the mechanism design literature, we formulate the optimal tax problem now as a two-dimensional screening problem. Unfortunately however, in contrast to many areas of economic theory where an increase in dimensionality simply involves a change in notation, an increase in the number of dimensions of private information in this mechanism design problem raises substantive issues.

The properties of the optimal taxation model for singles, with two wage types and one dimension of private information, are well understood and give a great deal of insight into the results of the more general case of n types, where n is arbitrarily large and may be defined on a continuum. The main limitations of the two-type case are: it cannot say anything about the shape of the optimal tax function, because only one type is subject to a positive MTR; it rules out

---

[24] This approach is adopted by Apps and Rees (2009) chs. 6 and 8, Brett (2007), Cremer et al. (2012), Kleven et al. (2009), and Schroyen (2003).

the possibility of 'bunching', where more than one type receives the same allocation of consumption and income; and it gives undue prominence to the 'no distortion at the top' result, which says that the MTR on the highest wage type is optimally zero, while not allowing consideration of the 'no distortion at the bottom' result which can also arise in the more general model.

The model closest to the two-type case has two persons in a household, each of whom may have one of two possible wage rates, implying that there are four possible household types. A number of authors have analysed versions of this model.[25] Here we summarise the model and results of the most comprehensive of these, that of Brett (2007).

4.1 Couples with Two Wage Types

The two wage earners $i = 1, 2$ in a household are identified as male and female and have wages drawn from the set $\{w_L, w_H\}$ with $0 < w_L < w_H$, and so a household of type $h \in \{LL, LH, HL, HH\}$ is now defined respectively by the pair

$$(w_1^h, w_2^h) \in \{(w_L, w_L), (w_L, w_H), (w_H, w_L), (w_H, w_H)\} \tag{36}$$

Each of the four household types has the additively separable utility function:

$$U_i^h = u(x_i^h) - v(y_i^h / w_i^h) \quad i = 1, 2 \tag{37}$$

where $u(.)$ and $v(.)$ are respectively strictly concave and convex and identical for all h, i. Here we formulate the model as if the planner allocates consumption and income quantities, but this is for analytical convenience. Underlying it is the fact that the planner can, on the assumptions of the model, induce a household to choose the optimal values of these variables by appropriate choice of the tax system. We also assume that the planner can identify to which household each individual belongs. The proportion of h-households in the economy is $\phi_h > 0$, and $\sum_h \phi_h = 1$.

Brett assumes that the household utility function is given by the 'collective' form:

$$U^h = u(x_h) - v(y_1^h / w_1^h) - \gamma v(y_2^h / w_2^h) \tag{38}$$

where $\gamma > 0$ is commonly interpreted as a measure of relative bargaining power, assumed exogenously fixed, equal for all households and known to the planner. Needless to say, this is a very strong assumption, though of course no stronger than the assumption that the planner also knows the utility function.

---

[25] See for example Apps and Rees (2009), Brett (2007) and Schroyen (2003). Mirrlees (1976) also discusses multidimensional screening problems in tax analysis.

In empirical family economics the household sharing rule which is equivalent to the value of γ, is a holy grail the search for which has generated a large literature. It appears that in only three countries, Denmark, the Netherlands and Japan, is data collected on within-household consumption allocations. See Browning and Gøtze (2012), Cherchye et al. (2012) and Lise and Yamada (2019). The assumption of additive separability in consumption and effort is standard in this type of adverse selection model, as is the assumption that both $u(.)$ and $v(.)$ are strictly increasing while the former is strictly concave and the latter strictly convex. Although this looks like a unitary utility function it can be derived from a 'collective' model by taking $u(x)$ to be the value function of the problem

$$\max_{x_i} U(x_1) + \gamma U(x_2) \ s.t. \sum_{i=1,2} x_i = x$$

More usually this household welfare function is given by the weighted utilitarian form

$$\alpha U(x_1) + (1 - a)U(x_2) \quad \alpha \in (0, 1)$$

The most important of the implications of these assumptions are:

Individual single crossing: At any interior point (y_i^0, x^0) in the (y_i, x)-plane, we have

$$\frac{\partial}{\partial w_i} \left[\frac{\partial v/\partial y_i}{\partial u/\partial x} \right] < 0 \ \ i = 1,2 \tag{39}$$

That is, the preferences of individuals satisfy the standard Spence-Mirrlees single crossing condition.

Decreasing utility difference: For any $(y^0, y^1) \in \mathbb{R}_+$ we have

$$v(y^1/w_L) - v(y^0/w_L) \geq v(y^1/w_H) - v(y^0/w_H) \geq 0 \Leftrightarrow y^1 \geq y^0 \tag{40}$$

with strict inequalities for $y'' > y'$. That is, the differences in utilities between any two earnings values are decreasing in the wage. This follows directly from the strict convexity of $v(.)$ in labour supply.

The key step in the mechanism design approach is the specification of the *IC* constraints. In the standard single individual household model with just two wage types this boils down simply to requiring the utility of the higher wage type to be at least as large when she truthfully reports her type as when she 'mimics' the lower wage type by falsely claiming to be that type. Given any allocation (x^0, y^0) designed for the low-wage type, incentive compatibility can always be achieved by requiring from the higher wage type a higher level of y while offering a higher level of x sufficient to make the overall (x, y)-bundle at least as attractive to her as (x^0, y^0), while not violating the other possible *IC* constraint, which rules out that the low-wage type would want to mimic the high wage type. In the standard model this latter constraint turns out to be non-binding at the optimum. Existence of this solution is guaranteed by the single crossing condition.

In Brett's 'two-person × two-wage' model, as we will now show, the formulation of the incentive compatibility constraints is much more complex and gives rise to far more solution possibilities in which different subsets of the constraint set are binding, resulting in a more complicated characterisation of the multiplicity of possible tax systems that may be optimal. The basic reason for this is the increase in the number of individual choice variables: there are now three for each household. In contrast to the one-dimensional case, in which the planner uses a lump sum tax and a single MTR to distort only the marginal rate of subsitution of the low-wage type, the planner now has three instruments, the MTR's on labour earnings of two individuals and the lump sum determining household consumption at given net wage rates. The MTR's are to be specified for each individual in each household, in order to control the household's marginal rates of substitution and give the desired labour supply distortions across the four household types. In all, twelve constraints are possible. We define

$$U^{hj} \equiv [u(x^j) - v(y_1^j/w_1^h) - \gamma v(y_2^j/w_2^h)] \tag{41}$$

$$U^{jh} \equiv [u(x^h) - v(y_1^h/w_1^j) - \gamma v(y_2^h/w_2^j)] \tag{42}$$

These give the utility household h (or j respectively) receives when it claims to be household j (or h respectively) for $h,j \in \{LL, LH, HL, HH\}$, $h \neq j$. It follows from (41) and (42) that all three *IC* constraints on any household h are simply given by

$$U^h \geq U^{hj} \text{ for } h,j \in \{LL, LH, HL, HH\}, h \neq j \tag{43}$$

The restrictions implied by incentive compatibility that can be placed on the allocations (x, y_1, y_2) the households receive can be derived by specifying the relevant types h,j summing the resulting constraint pairs and finally applying the decreasing utility difference result. Here we simply summarise the main results and provide some intuition.

The four possible pairs of households $\{HH, LH\}, \{HH, HL\}, \{LH, LL\}$, and $\{HL, LL\}$ have one and only one type in common, respectively individual two in the first, one in the second, one in the third and two in the fourth. Holding one type constant, so to speak, the other types fall into the standard pattern of the *IC* constraints in the one-dimensional model. This suggests that we can apply the intuition from that model. Consider the first pair. The planner could require that $y_1^{HH} \geq y_1^{LH}, y_2^{HH} > y_2^{LH}$, and ensure incentive compatibility with sufficient inequality in consumptions with $x^{HH} > x^{LH}$ to compensate for the higher effort level of at least one of the higher productivity types. This would also work if $y_1^{HH} > y_1^{LH}, y_2^{HH} \geq y_2^{LH}$. Moreover, the same argument applies for the pairs $\{HH, HL\}, \{LH, LL\}$ and $\{HL, LL\}$. From this we see immediately that incentive compatibility does not rule out any of the following possibilities:

(i) different treatment for the two individuals in a household even when they are of the same type;

(ii) different treatment of the same type in different households;

(iii) the treatment received by a given type depends on the type of their partner in the household;

(iv) a 'top type' H can have a distortion of its labour supply.

In the case of the households $\{HH, LL\}$, we have the possible result that $y_i^{HH} < y_i^{LL} \Rightarrow y_j^{HH} > y_j^{LL}$ $i, j = 1, 2, i \neq j$. That is, incentive compatibility does not now rule out the possibility that one partner in the high productivity household could be required to earn less than the corresponding low productivity partner in the other household (which cannot happen of course in a unidimensional model) as long as the other partner has to earn more, to avoid the LL household mimicking the HH household.

Finally, in the case of the households $\{HL, LH\}, \{LH, LL\}$ we have similar possibilities that could not arise in a unidimensional model: incentive compatibility does not rule out the results: $y_1^{HL} < y_1^{LH} \Rightarrow y_2^{LH} > y_2^{HL}$ with $x^{LH} > x^{HL}$; and $y_2^{LH} < y_2^{HL} \Rightarrow y_1^{HL} > y_1^{LH}$ with $x^{LH} > x^{HL}$. In each of these cases again a high productivity individual in one household is required to earn less than the corresponding low productivity individual in the other, as long as incentive compatibility is maintained by choice of the other two instruments.

We now consider the planner's optimal tax system.

The SWF in the problem:

$$S = S(U^{LL}, U^{LH}, U^{HL}, U^{HH}) \tag{44}$$

is defined on household rather than individual utilities. This avoids the issue that if the SWF defined on individual utilities differs from the household's utility function in the welfare weights given to individuals then the solution to the optimal tax problem will in general have terms relating to the attempted correction of this by the planner in the direction of their own preference. Here tax policy is concerned only with the allocation of resources among households, implicitly accepting whatever within-household allocation the household decides upon.

$S(.)$ is to be maximised subject to:

(i) a standard resource constraint: aggregate consumption must equal aggregate production:

$$\sum_h \phi_h \left[y_1^h + y_2^h - x^h \right] = 0 \tag{45}$$

and

(ii) the set of *IC* constraints given above. The Lagrangian is therefore

$$\mathcal{L} = S(.) + \lambda \sum_h \phi_h(y_1^h + y_2^h - x^h) + \sum_h \sum_{,j \neq h} \mu_j^h(U^h - U_j^h] \tag{46}$$

for $h, j \in \{LL, LH, HL, HH\}$, $h \neq j$. The following first order conditions characterise an interior global optimum:

$$\left[S^h + \sum_{j \neq h} (\mu_j^h - \mu_h^j) \right] u'(x^h) - \lambda \phi_h = 0 \quad h, j \in \{LL, HL, LH, HH\} \tag{47}$$

$$\left(S^h + \sum_{j \neq h} \mu_j^h \right) \frac{v'(y_2^h/w_2^h)}{w_i^h} - \sum_{j \neq h} \mu_h^j \frac{\gamma v'(y_2^h/w_2^h)}{w_i^j} + \lambda \phi_h = 0 \tag{48}$$

for $i = 1, 2$ $h, j \in \{LL, HL, LH, HH\}$, with S^h the welfare weight attached to household h at the optimum. It is straightforward to show that $\lambda > 0$ at the optimum, given nonsatiation – any excess of output over consumption could always be distributed lump sum, and consumption can never exceed output in the aggregate. The exact pattern of binding *IC* constraints, with $\mu_j^h > 0$, determines the optimal tax structure.

The following results can be shown to hold.[26] It is useful to express these results in terms of marginal tax rates, which are of course derived from the first order conditions for the solution to this problem. The tax rate t_i^h $h \in \{LL, LH, HL, HH\}$, $i = 1, 2$, gives the marginal tax rate on individual i in household h. Then:

1. The four L-type earners in the households $h \in \{LL, LH, HL\}$ face tax rates $t_1^{LL}, t_2^{LL}, t_1^{LH}, t_2^{HL} \geq 0$
2. $t_1^{LL} > 0$ *iff* at least one of $\mu_{LL}^{HL}, \mu_{LL}^{HH} > 0$; $t_2^{LL} > 0$ *iff* at least one of μ_{LL}^{LH}, $\mu_{LL}^{HH} > 0$
3. $t_1^{LH} > 0$ *iff* at least one of $\mu_{LL}^{HL}, \mu_{LL}^{HH} > 0$; $t_2^{HL} > 0$ *iff* at least one of μ_{LL}^{LH}, $\mu_{LL}^{HH} > 0$
4. The H-type earners in the households $h \in \{LH, HL, HH\}$ face tax rates $t_i^h \leq 0$, $i = 1, 2$;
5. $t_1^{HL} < 0$ *iff* at least one of $\mu_{HL}^{LH}, \mu_{HL}^{LL} > 0$; $t_2^{LH} < 0$ *iff* at least one of μ_{LL}^{HL}, $\mu_{LL}^{LL} > 0$
6. $t_1^{HH} < 0$ *iff* at least one of $\mu_{HL}^{LH}, \mu_{HL}^{LL} > 0$; $t_2^{HH} < 0$ *iff* $\mu_{HL}^{LH}, \mu_{HL}^{LL} > 0$.

Thus low-wage individuals cannot receive subsidies, and whether or not their tax rates are positive depends on the precise configuration of their incentive

---

[26] See Proposition 7 in Brett (2007) for a lengthy discussion of the derivation of these results.

compatibility constraints with the other households. High-wage individuals cannot have positive tax rates and whether or not they receive subsidies again depends on the precise configuration of their incentive compatibilty constraints with the other households.

The basic intuition here is that distorting the labour supply of an individual only relaxes an incentive constraint in a situation in which single crossing holds in the relevant (y_i,x)-plane with strictly binding constraints. This can happen only when y_i^h and y_i^j are of different wage types. When they are of the same wage type there is no single crossing and therefore no gain from distorting their choices. So an individual of given type in any household will only face a distortion, whether achieved by means of a tax or subsidy, when at the optimum the relevant constraint, is strictly binding. This implies of course that the pattern of binding constraints determines the structure of the tax system, and many corresponding tax systems may result.

One striking aspect of these results is the possibility of negative tax rates – subsidies – to high wage types. This simply reflects the possibility that distorting the effort supply of a high wage type upward relaxes an IC constraint by making mimicking of one household by another less attractive: the low-wage earner in the would-be mimicking household would have to supply even more effort to mimic the high-wage earner in the household it seeks to mimic. Recall that the role of the marginal tax rates in this kind of model is to control labour supplies; to deal with the adverse distributive implications of such subsidies there is always the lump sum tax/subsidy aspect of the tax system, which can come into play because self-selection is satisfied and so type is fully identified.

Brett derives a number of further results based on one or both of the assumptions that the distribution of types is uniform, so that the ϕ_h are all equal, and that the household utility functions are quasilinear. Space constraints require that we leave the study of these to the interested reader.

Cremer et al. (2012) provide a useful complement to Brett (2007) by showing that when the assumption of only two possible wage types is relaxed, thus allowing for an arbitrarily large number of couple households, it is possible to prove that it is still highly unlikely that joint taxation would be optimal. This is because in their setting it is not guaranteed that income taxes on women should be lower than those on men. They avoid the complexities that Brett had to face, which of course are exponentially increasing in the number of households, by assuming perfect assortative matching. They also show that in this setting not only the differences in labour supply elasticities, but also the intricate way in which productivity differences between individuals within and across households interact with *IC* constraints, make it difficult to determine the relationship between the optimal taxes on each individual in each household type. This is in general so complex that the authors resort to a specific (additively separable and isoelastic) form for the household utility functions to enable them to show that French (though not US) data support the argument that women should face higher marginal tax rates than men. The results are of course contingent on a Mirrlees-type taxation system, with its associated structure of lump sum payments, being in existence. Therefore it is hard to say how the results would apply to a real-world, piecewise linear tax system.

4.2 Taxation at the Intensive and Extensive Margins

In the theory of the optimal taxation of singles a literature has developed emphasising the distinction between taxation at the extensive margin, which influences the decision of whether to supply labour to the market or not, and taxation at the intensive margin, which influences the number of hours worked. This has arisen at least in part out of concern with public policies to deal with issues at the lower end of the income distribution. For example in the US and UK there are policies designed to support low-wage individuals by supplementing their in-work earnings, but only if they do have jobs.

In the Mirrlees framework, low-income individuals are poor because they have low innate ability, and in some versions of the model they are optimally subject to high marginal rates of taxation, possibly even high enough to exclude them from the labour market altogether. To correct the impression of an apparent lack of social concern in such a policy it should yet again be stressed that in the Mirrlees framework marginal tax rates are simply instruments to induce socially optimal labour supply decisions, and the lump sum component of the system can be used to support the living standard of highly taxed low-ability workers. Nonetheless this view conflicts with the school of thought which opposes high social transfers for low-ability workers. The justification is that it allows higher-ability workers to be taxed more heavily by reducing the extent to which they find it worthwhile to mimic lower-earning individuals in order to avoid taxes, thus supporting the aims of income redistribution. The starkest example of this is in the two-type case, where completely excluding the low-wage type would ensure that the only type remaining in the market is the higher wage type, who can then be taxed mercilessly by an optimal lump sum tax. This case can be optimal under certain parameter constellations. It is natural therefore that the Mirrlees approach has been extended to take account of family taxation at both the extensive and intensive margins. In this subsection we survey the resulting literature.

Kleven et al. (2009) analyse a model with a double continuum of household types. For each primary earner's wage w defined on the interval

$[w_{\min}, w_{\max}] \subset \mathbb{R}_{++}$, there is a continuum of second earners defined with respect to a variable $q \in \mathbb{R}_+$ which represents, in one version of the model, fixed costs of going out to work, and in another, the value of household production foregone. Of course, in reality both of these are likely to exist in any household with a second earner. By assuming that each second earner's labour supply is the result of a binary participation decision between not working on the market, or taking a job with a given, observable income that is the same for all second earners, they transform this two-dimensional screening problem into one involving two related one-dimensional problems. This is important to the solution of the model.

Primary earners' types are, as in the standard Mirrlees model, defined by their innate productivities or unobservable wage rates, while second earners may enter the workforce or not. If they do, they earn the income $y > 0$, which is the same for all and is public information. They participate in the labour market if and only if the household is at least as well off as if they stayed at home, taking into account taxes and their value of q. In both versions of the model there are then two subsets of households at each primary wage, those in which the second earner supplies labour to the market and observably adds y to the gross household income, and those in which she does not. Thus the household's choice of primary earners' labour supply is along the intensive margin, second earners' only at the extensive margin.

Tax rates are applied to the primary earner's income but differ at each primary wage type according to whether the second earner is in the workforce or not. The difference between the tax rates for primary earners with the same wage but different participation decisions for their partners is an implicit redistributive participation tax or subsidy. The aim is to establish the nature of the optimal jointness between the primary earner's wage and this implicit participation tax/subsidy: how should the tax function for primary earners depend upon the participation decision of the second earner as we move through the primary wage distribution? Note that the joint vs individual income does not arise: the focus of the analysis has changed to optimal jointness.

The answer to this question will depend on which type of household, at any given primary wage, is better off, the one in which the second earner works in the market or the one in which she does not, because this determines the direction in which the planner will want to transfer utility and income – towards or away from the single-earner household.

Take first the model where q is a fixed cost of work. Since households with the same primary wage are identical except for the value of q, in the absence of taxes second earners who go out to work belong to households with $q \leq y$. These are therefore better off than those with the same primary earner wage but no second earner labour supply. This means that, given a conventional SWF, the planner will want to redistribute at each primary wage from the households with an in-work second earner to those without.

In the second proposed model, the variable q is interpreted as a productivity in the household production foregone if she works in the market. Again she will be in the workforce if and only if this makes the household better off, but now, in the absence of taxation such households must be the ones with lower domestic productivity, which are therefore all strictly worse off than households choosing non-participation, which have $q > y$. Thus redistribution will take place in the opposite direction, from single-earner to two-earner households.

Note that this does however raise the question, considered by the authors in a website appendix, of what happens when both costs of work and household production are present, particularly, as they say, 'the two types of heterogeneity pull optimal redistribution policy in opposite directions'. It could be therefore that a tax system with zero jointness may be a better approximation to the optimum after all.

For reasons of space, we focus here on the former model. The main result is that, given a number of assumptions discussed below, jointness is optimally negative: The implicit participation tax rate on the second earner is lower the higher the primary wage. This is an apparently regressive and on the face of it somewhat counter-intuitive result: progressivity in taxation would seem to imply positive jointness. In this model however, since all in-work second earners have the same income, the negative jointness result has a surprisingly simple intuitive rationalisation given the assumptions of the model. The mathematical complexities in the paper arise in formulating the conditions that ensure it holds. We discuss these once we have briefly set out the model more formally.

Households have the quasilinear indirect utility function:[27]

$$V_\delta(w) = y_\delta(w) + (y - q)\delta - T_\delta(y_\delta(w)) - wg\left(\frac{y_\delta(w)}{w}\right) \tag{49}$$

$$\delta \in \{0, 1\}; \quad w \in [w_{\min}, w_{\max}] \subset \mathbb{R}_{++}; \quad q \in (0, \infty); \quad \frac{y_\delta}{w} \in [0, 1]; \quad g' > 0, g'' > 0$$

Here y_δ and w are the primary earner gross income and wage type respectively, $\delta \in \{0, 1\}$ is the binary participation variable. A household's type is given by the pair (w, q). The tax function on primary earners conditional on δ is $T_\delta(y_\delta(w))$ and $wg(.)$ is a cost of effort function for primary earners. Underlying this is an optimal labour supply choice: The utility function is $U_l = c_l - wh(y_l/w)$ with household consumption $c_l = y_l + (y - q)l - T_l(y_l)$. In the absence of taxation the primary earner's labour supply is independent of the spouse's participation

---

[27] Kleven et al. define V_1 as not containing q, which simplifies some aspects of their presentation but is unnecessary here, so we use the more natural formulation.

decision but will adapt to differential taxation via the tax function $T_l(.)$ for primary earners with first order condition $g'(y_\delta(w)/w) = 1 - T'_\delta(y_l(w))$. We denote by $\bar{q}(w)$ the value of q at which $V_1(w) = V_0(w)$, thus defining the marginal household with a participating second earner. Clearly at any primary wage w the value of $\bar{q}$ depends on the tax system, as well as on the density function of q, conditioned on the primary earner wage type and defined as $p(q \mid w)$, while $f(w)$ is the density function for primary wage types. $P(q \mid w)$ and $F(w)$ are the corresponding cumulative distribution functions.

The planner maximises:

$$\int_{w_1^{\min}}^{w_1^{\max}} \int_0^\infty \Psi(V_\delta(w)) p(q \mid w) f(w) dq dw$$

with the SWF $\Psi(.)$, $\Psi' > 0, \Psi'' < 0$.

The formulation of the model described makes clear that the problem is to find two different but related optimal non-linear tax functions of the Mirrlees type, and the paper proves that the solution functions indeed possess the standard properties of such functions, which, on the important assumption of no bunching, include the 'no distortion at the top' and 'no distortion at the bottom' results. For this they need a regularity condition on the cost of effort function: $[1 - h'(x)]/[x[h''(x)]$ is strictly decreasing in x. This ensures that the optimal tax functions achieve a maximum rather than a minimum and is satisfied by a reasonable range of functions, for example the CRRA form $h(x) = x^{1+1/\varepsilon}/(1 + 1/\varepsilon)$. Thus, across all households with the same participation decision, the usual kind of redistribution from more to less productive primary earners takes place.

The paper aims to establish the negative jointness result. The two tax functions correspond to $T_1(y_1(w))$ and $T_0(y_0(w))$ with marginal tax rates $T'_\delta(y_l(w)) \in (0, 1)$, and zero at the end-points (given no bunching). Since at any given $w \in [w_1^{\min}, w_1^{\max}]$, the planner wants to redistribute from two-earner to single earner households, the former tax function lies everywhere above the latter. The vertical distance between them is the implicit participation tax. Then, if this tax is monotonically decreasing as we move upward through the wage distribution, we must have at every $\hat{w} \in (w_1^{\min}, w_1^{\max})$ that $T'_1(y_1(\hat{w})) < T'_0(y_0(\hat{w}))$, so that at each primary earner wage type, except the end-points, the marginal tax rate on primary earners in two-earner households is always strictly less than that in single-earner households. Of course, this does not make the tax bill of the two-earner households lower, since at each w they also pay a lump sum tax which ensures that their overall tax burden is higher.

To obtain negative jointness the paper makes a number of additional assumptions, which are:

- The density $p(.)$ is independent of n, so there is no association between the primary earner's wage type and the second earner's fixed cost of work. This greatly simplifies the analysis of what happens to the subsets of households when we move along the optimal tax functions as the primary earner wage type changes.
- The function $qp(w - q)/[P(w - q)(1 - P(w - q)]$ is increasing in q; and $p(q)/P(q) \leq P(q)/\int_0^q P(q')dq'$
- $\Psi''' > 0$, marginal social utility is strictly convex in $V(w)$.

There is a simple intuition underlying these assumptions and the negative jointness result. $\Psi''(V_\delta(w))$ corresponds to the assumed strictly convex marginal social utility of income function, which reflects the weight that the planner places on the well-being of each type of household as we move through the wage distribution. As in any standard optimal tax model, the extent of the redistribution from one type to another depends *inter al.* on the sign and magnitude of the differences in their values of marginal social utility. Consider the pair of households whose utilities are denoted by V_0^1, V_1^1. These are assumed to represent households with the same primary earner wage. By assumption, V_0^1 is the utility level of a household with $\delta = 0$ and V_1^1 that of a household with $\delta = 1$. Then $\Delta\Psi_1'$ is the difference in their marginal social utility weights and implies a redistribution from two-earner to single-earner households.

Suppose for simplicity that as we move through the entire primary wage distribution the differences $V_1 - V_0$ are non-increasing, as are the proportions of households in each of the two subsets (this is stronger than strictly necessary: increasing differences have to be sufficiently small not to at least offset the convexity of the marginal social utility function). Then obviously, the strict convexity of marginal social utility implies that $\Delta\Psi'$ is falling, and this would hold for all pairs of household types with the same primary wage but differing second earner participation. The force of the first two of the assumptions, intuitively speaking, is to ensure that the differences in the (V_0, V_1) pairs are not sufficient to offset the effect of the convexity of marginal social utility curve as we move through the primary earner wage distribution. Intuitively, for negative jointness, for each successive pair (V_0, V_1) the differences in utilities $V_1 - V_0$ in conjunction with the degree of convexity of the $\Psi'(V(w))$-function and the relative proportions of the two types must always be such as to generate a smaller difference in welfare weights and hence in marginal tax rates $T_0'(y_1(w)) - T_1'(y_0(w))$.

The main question concerning these results is that of how they can be applied to real tax systems, given the assumption that second earners' labour supply choices take place only at the extensive margin, and involve a fixed number of working hours at the same, observable wage for all. From the purely technical point of view, this gets rid of the problem of the large multiplicity of the sets of possibly binding incentive compatibility constraints that we saw in the previous discussion of the Brett model. Here we simply have two standard *IC* constraints on single-earner and two-earner households respectively.

Assuming away the intensive margin for second earners is however a very strong, counterfactual assumption. In reality women as second earners are much more elastic in their choices at both the intensive and extensive margins than male primary earners, and there is far more part-time work by women as second earners than by men, as well as much more variation across the hours distribution. It is therefore unclear as to what insight the analysis gives into the problem of how to tax women or second earners more generally at their intensive margin.

This is even more problematic when we take into account the empirical evidence showing that average second-earner incomes are *increasing* with primary-earner incomes. The gap between marginal social utilities of single and two-earner households is in that case increasing, and it is easy to see that this could more than offset the convexity of the $\Psi'(V(w))$-function and so reverse the 'negative jointness' result. So the intensive margin for second earners does matter.

Finally, the paper shows that in the case where q represents the value of foregone household production when the second earner goes out to work, single earner households are those with values of household production higher than the market wage, in which case these are the better off households and the previous conclusions are precisely reversed. In reality, second earners will face both fixed costs of work and foregone household production, in which the direction of jointness, whether positive or negative, is indeterminate. In that case, who is to say that the assumption of (approximately) zero jointness is not a better approximation than either of the two extremes? Thus a piecewise linear model could be superior.

4.3 Double-Extensive Margins

The paper by Immervoll et al. (2011) follows on directly from Kleven et al. (2009), with the difference that it is concerned with participation taxes on *both* male and female partners. We present here a brief outline of the main theoretical part of the paper.

The set of couple households is partitioned into three non-empty subsets, indexed $j = 0, 1, 2$. In the first, neither partner participates in the labour market, in the second, only the primary earner participates and in the third both earners participate. The innate ability of primary earners, the same for all,[28] is w_1, and with working hours normalised at 1 (no intensive margin) this is also the earnings from the labour supply of all primary earners. Likewise there is only one w_2 for the second earner. The assumption that there is only one household wage type is the only simplification we make to the model, which has an arbitrary but finite number H of wage types. It simplifies the presentation without losing anything of substance. Since earnings are observable and work hours are fixed innate ability is also observable, that is, there is no multidimensional screening problem. The number of households of type j is ϕ_j, and the total number of households is $\sum_j \phi_j = 1$. Thus there are two extensive margins, for primary and second earners respectively. This model structure is based on Saez (2002), which dealt with single-earner households. That paper was concerned with analysing the question of whether low-ability workers should be given wage subsidies to induce them to participate, motivated by policy innovations of this type in the US and UK.

In the absence of taxation, households have quasilinear utility functions defined on consumption, given by earnings less work costs c_i:

$$u_0 = 0; \; u_1 = w_1 - c_1; \; u_2 = \sum_{i=1,2}(w_i - c_i) \tag{50}$$

This rules out income effects. The fixed costs of work $c_i \in \mathbb{R}_+$, $i = 1, 2$, are the key exogenous variables that drive the analysis. They are distributed across households with the exogenously given joint probability distribution $F(c_1, c_2)$. For primary earners, the marginal distribution and density functions are $F_1(c_1)$ and $f_1(c_1) \equiv F_1'(c_1)$ respectively. In any equilibrium there is a strictly positive and finite pair of values $\bar{c}_1, \bar{c}_2$ such that a necessary condition for participation is that $c_i \leq \bar{c}_i$, $i = 1, 2$. With the help of some additional assumptions, this generates the three subsets: no one participates; only the primary earner participates; both earners participate. This excludes the possibility that households exist in which only the second earner participates, which is why the additional assumptions are required.

Households are assumed to take sequential participation decisions: first they decide whether the primary earner participates, and *only if* this decision is to participate, do they then take the participation decision for the second earner. Given this assumption, the probability that a second earner participates is conditional on whether the primary earner does. Thus for second earners we have the conditional distribution function $F_{21}(c_2 \mid c_1)$ for each $c_1 \leq \bar{c}_1$. The possibilities that only second earners participate, and that a two-earner participating

---

[28] As before, the notation is that used throughout this Element rather than that of the paper discussed.

household can switch to being a non-participating household and conversely, are ruled out. Given this, changes in tax rates can only cause households to switch between non-participation and primary-earner subsets on the one hand, or between primary-earner and two-earner subsets on the other.

It follows that the numbers of households in each subset are given by:

$$\phi_0 = [1 - F_1(\bar{c}_1)]; \quad \phi_1 = F(\bar{c}_1) - \phi_2; \phi_2 = \int_0^{\bar{c}_1} F_{21}(\bar{c}_2 \mid c_1) dF_1 \tag{51}$$

The critical values $\bar{c}_i$ are determined once we specify the tax system. The planner's instruments are lump sum taxes $T_0, T_1, T_2 \in \mathbb{R}$ set respectively for the households with zero, one or two earners. At least for households in which nobody participates we must have $T_0 < 0$ if they are to have $u_0 > 0$. From (51) we have:

$$u_0 = -T_0; \quad u_1 = w_1 - c_1 - T_1; \quad u_2 = \sum_{i=1,2} (w_i - c_i) - T_2 \tag{52}$$

The necessary conditions for only single-earner participation and two-earner participation are respectively:

$$u_1 \geq u_0; u_2 \geq u_1 \tag{53}$$

The critical values $\bar{c}_i$ are therefore defined respectively by:

$$\bar{c}_1 \equiv w_1 - (T_1 - T_0) \tag{54}$$

and, conditionally on $u_1 \geq u_0$ by:

$$\bar{c}_2 \equiv w_2 - (T_2 - T_1) \tag{55}$$

Note that if we instead impose the unconditional requirement:

$$\bar{c}_2 \equiv w_2 - (T_1 - T_0) \tag{56}$$

we have the possibility that households exist in which in which $c_1 > \bar{c}_1$ and $c_2 < \bar{c}_2$ so that only the second earner would participate. The paper argues that such a possibility introduces technical complications that are better avoided, and so assumes that the nature of the joint probability distribution is such that these cases have zero probability of occurring. To ensure formally that the case where only the second earner participates is ruled out we need two further critical values, which we denote by c_1^L, c_2^L. Perhaps the quickest way to define these is to show the role they play in the formulation of the planner's objective function. We now turn to this.

We formulate the planner's problem in terms of the lump sum taxes as follows. The planner's budget constraint is simply $\sum_{j=0,1,2} \phi_j T_j \geq R$, where $R \geq 0$ is a per capita revenue requirement. The formulation of the planner's SWF S

takes a little more work. First, welfare weights $\omega(c_1, c_2)$ are assigned to every household since, given the assumptions on wage rates, c_1, c_2 are, in conjunction with taxes, essentially what determine household utility (recall that households are better off the lower are these fixed costs so desired redistribution is towards households with higher costs). Then the first of the three components of the SWF is:

$$\Omega_0 = \int_{\bar{c}_1}^{\infty} \int_{c_2^L(c_1)}^{\infty} \omega(c_1, c_2) u_0(c_1, c_2) dF \tag{57}$$

where $F(c_1, c_2)$ is the joint distribution of work costs over the entire population of households and $c_2^L(c_1)$, given the critical value c_2^L as a function of c_1, is sufficiently high that no second earner wants to participate. These then are the households with both individuals non-participating.

The second component of S is:

$$\Omega_1 = \int_{c_1^L}^{\bar{c}_1} \int_{c_2^L(c_1)}^{\infty} \omega(c_1, c_2) u_0(c_1, c_2) dF \tag{58}$$

$$+ \int_0^{c_1^L} \int_{\bar{c}_2}^{\infty} \omega(c_1, c_2) u_0(c_1, c_2) dF \tag{59}$$

In order to ensure that only primary earners want to participate we have to choose a lower limit c_1^L of the first integral such that all primary earners with costs in the interval $(c_1^L, \bar{c}_1)$ want to work but again for all c_1 in that interval second earners are in the interval $(c_2^L(c_1), \infty)$ and so do not want to participate. In the second term we have those second earners with costs higher than the critical level $\bar{c}_2$ who therefore do not want to work, while their spouses in the interval $\bar{c}_2(0, c_2^L(c_1))$ do, since $c_2^L(c_1) < \bar{c}_1$.

The final component of S is:

$$\Omega_2 = \int_0^{c_1^L} \int_{c_2^L(c_1)}^{\bar{c}_2} \omega(c_1, c_2) u_0(c_1, c_2) dF \tag{60}$$

The interval over which the second integral is taken, $(c_2^L, \bar{c}_2)$ refers to those second earners who want to work, with a zero probability of their having a lower cost than $c_2^L(c_1)$ for all $c_1 \in (0, c_1^L)$

Then the Lagrangian for the planner's problem is

$$\mathcal{L} = \sum_{j=0,1,2} \Omega_j + \lambda \left(\sum_{j=0,1,2,} \phi_j T_j - R \right) \tag{61}$$

To emphasise the nature of this problem as a linear tax problem, we define:

$$t_1 \equiv \frac{T_1 - T_0}{w_1}; \quad t_2 \equiv \frac{T_2 - T_1}{w_2} \tag{62}$$

as the optimal tax *rates*. The first order conditions for this problem then yield:

$$\frac{t_1}{1-t_1} = \frac{1-g_1}{\eta_1} + \frac{1-g_2}{\eta_1}\frac{\phi_2}{\phi_1} \tag{63}$$

$$\frac{t_2}{1-t_2} = \frac{1-g_2}{\eta_2} \quad h = 1,,,,,h \tag{64}$$

where g_j is the average of the marginal social utilities of income across the subset of households $j = 1,2$, the single and two-earner households respectively, and

$$\eta_j \equiv \frac{\partial \phi_j}{\partial(1-t_j)}\frac{(1-t_j)}{\phi_j} > 0 \quad j = 1,2 \tag{65}$$

is the elasticity of the number of households in subset j with respect to the retention rate. The '1' in the numerator terms of the expressions (63) and (64) results from the well-known fact that in the absence of income effects, the average of the marginal social utility of a lump sum transfer across the entire population is 1, which is also the marginal cost of the transfer. In this model it is as if the planner made a lump sum transfer to all households – the demogrant – and then recoups it with a tax on the wage earnings of the better off households.

Thus, $1 - g_j$ gives the difference between the population average and the average for subsector j. Since the two-earner households are the most well off in this economy (have the highest labour earnings) $1 - g_2 > 0$ for sure and so they will definitely pay a tax. Single-earner households will have (in the absence of income effects) a lower value $1 - g_1 \gtrless 0$. Thus, for equal values of η_j we can interpret the difference $t_2 - t_1$ as a participation tax on the second earner. So, just as in any other linear tax system, we can interpret the numerator in the expression as the distributional element in the tax. The denominator is the efficiency element. An increase in t_2 relative to t_1 will cause the second earners with the highest fixed costs in this subset to drop out, which of course reduces total output.

Turning now to the result for t_1, the presence of the second term involving the net marginal social utility of second earners is due to the restriction that participating second earners belong to a subset of participating primary earners, so that a change in the number of primary earners also changes the number of second earners – a second earner cannot be left without a participating partner. The first term of course is just the direct effect on primary earners. The intuition for these results is precisely that of optimal linear taxation once we adjust for the fact that the only margin is the extensive one.

The paper goes on to introduce income effects into the unitary model, and then analyses a collective model without and with income effects. Space precludes full discussion of these, which in any case do little to change the basic form of the results, but we will comment briefly on the results for the collective model. The main formal result is that the expressions for the welfare weights have to be adjusted to take into account the fact that there may be dissonance between the planner's welfare weights placed on the individuals within a household and those of the household itself. Through the tax system the planner seeks to nudge the household in her preferred direction. One important conclusion the authors derive is:

> The bottom line is that, if income effects are small and in the absence of empirical evidence on third-order properties of utility functions, income taxation is not a useful instrument to deal with intra-household equity issues. In this case, the design of income taxation should focus on inter-household equity issues, a question that can be analyzed adequately based on the much simpler unitary approach.

This is directly relevant to the discussion of the next paper we consider.

4.4 Within Household Inequality

None of the models considered up until now have focused on the implications of possible inequality of well-being between the members of a couple household for the design of the optimal non-linear tax system. Though Brett's model contained the within-household distributional parameter γ, beyond allowing for asymmetry in the allocations of household members it did not play an explicit role in the analysis. Also, as just noted, Immervoll et al. also studied the case of the collective household. In Cremer et al. (2016), on the other hand, this becomes the main object of analysis. Their household model is basically that of Brett (2007), but with two important generalisations and two important restrictions. The generalisations are that there is an arbitrary number H of household types indexed $h = 1, 2, ..., H$ (as in Cremer et al. (2012)), and that the bargaining weights, assumed the same for all households by Brett, are here free to vary across households, in a way that depends on wage rates. Collective models typically assume that an individual's weight increases with her wage rate relative to that of her partner. See for example Apps and Rees (1988, 2009) and Lise and Seitz (2011). These are expressed as is usual in collective models by a weight attached to each individual utility function, rather than a single value corresponding to their ratio, as in Brett. Here they play a much more important role.

The restrictions are, first, that there is perfect assortative matching: we have

$$w_i^{h+1} > w_i^h \ i = 1, 2, \forall h$$

Thus the screening problem is essentially one-dimensional. Secondly, in the calculation of numerical examples, the individuals are assumed to have constant, identical labour supply elasticities. Both these assumptions are made in order to capture the effects of the dissonance between the planner's and the households' welfare weights more sharply.

The household utility functions take the form:

$$U = \sum_{i=1,2} \alpha_i [u(x_i) - v(y_i/w_i)] \tag{66}$$

where $\alpha_i \in (0,1)$, $\sum_{i=1,2} \alpha_i = 1$ are the individual weights. It is also assumed that $w_1 > w_2$, there is a gender wage gap.

In the absence of taxation, the assumptions of additive separability and identical utility functions in this household model make it very easy to analyse. Given the household's Lagrange function:

$$\mathcal{L} = U + \lambda \sum_{i=1,2} (y_i - x_i) \tag{67}$$

The first order conditions are simply:

$$u'(x_i) = \lambda/\alpha_i \ i = 1,2 \tag{68}$$

$$v'(y_i/w_i) = \lambda w_i/\alpha_i \ \ i = 1,2 \tag{69}$$

implying that

$$\frac{v'(y_1/w_1)}{v'(y_2/w_2)} = \frac{w_1}{w_2} \frac{\alpha_2}{\alpha_1} \tag{70}$$

so that if $\alpha_1 > \alpha_2$, the household acts as if the wage gap between the two earners in a household is lower than it really is, and could even be negative, *iff* $w_1/w_2 < \alpha_1/\alpha_2$. Thus, relative to the case where the weights are equal, given that labour supply is strictly increasing in the wage the female supplies too much time to the labour market and the male too little.

Finally, note that the planner is assumed not to be able to observe individual consumptions, and so she has to solve the problem[29]:

$$\max_{x_i^h} \sum_{i=1,2} \alpha_i u(x_i^h) \ \text{s.t.} \ \sum_{i=1,2} x_i = x^h \ \ h = 1,...,H \tag{71}$$

For any given x^h the value function of this problem is $\sum_{i=1,2} \alpha_i v_i^h(x^h)$, and this can then be used in the optimal tax problem. It is easy to show from the comparative statics of this problem that $\partial x_i^h/\partial x^h > 0, \forall h, i = 1,2$.

The results of this model are quite dramatic: The utilitarian planner attaches equal welfare weights of 1 on all individuals while the households have unequal weights $\alpha_1^h > \alpha_2^h, \forall h$. Then an optimal tax system will involve terms that seek

---

[29] We now reintroduce the h superscript.

to shift the achieved consumption levels within each household closer toward equality, and to have a higher male and lower female labour supply, implying lower male and higher female leisure. The authors assume that this is done by what they call Pigou taxes (following Immervoll et al. (2011), the planner will want to put a Pigou tax on women and give a Pigou subsidy to men. The paper then shows that when this is incorporated into the Mirrlees tax model the Pigou tax is added to a standard Mirrlees incentive tax. Then, a positive tax on the female and a negative tax on the male are possible outcomes.

Anyone familiar with the empirical evidence on male and female labour supplies might find this surprising, since in OECD countries on average about one-third of women have a zero market labour supply and the average female working hours are significantly lower than those of males.[30] However, the logic of the model says that however low (but positive) the number of hours women work in the market, this is too high from the point of view of the planner, given that $\alpha_1^h > \alpha_2^h, \forall h$.

We now summarise the formal tax analysis very briefly. Since the planner is utilitarian, the optimal tax problem in the absence of asymmetric information is to choose x^h, y_i^h to maximise the SWF:

$$S = \sum_h \phi_h \sum_{i=1,2} \alpha_i^h [v_i^h(x^h) - v(y_i^h/w_i^h)] \tag{72}$$

The planner's resource constraint is again

$$\sum_h \phi_h [y_1^h + y_2^h - x^h] = 0 \tag{73}$$

It must be assumed that the planner knows not only the distribution of wage pairs but also the weights α_i^h that are associated with each wage pair in the distribution, or at least the functions that generate them from the wage rates.

The IC constraints are therefore:

$$\sum_{i=1,2} \alpha_i^h [v_i^h(x^h) - v(y_i^h/w_i^h)] \geq \sum_{i=1,2} \alpha_i^h [v_i^h(x^j) - v(y_i^j/w_i^h)] \quad h, j = 1, .., H, \ h \neq j \tag{74}$$

We give the results of the analysis in three steps. First, suppose that wage rates are observable, so *IC* constraints are unnecessary. We then have what Cremer et al. call a pure Pigovian problem. From the first order conditions from the

---

[30] The non-participation of women is not addressed in this paper but it is addressed in Immervoll et al. (2011).

problem involving only the resource constraint, the paper shows that we have the Pigou taxes[31]:

$$t_i^{Ph} = \left(1 - \frac{\alpha_i^h}{\alpha_k^h}\right) \frac{\partial x_i^h}{\partial x^h} \quad i,k = 1,2, \ i \neq k \tag{75}$$

It follows that the female's Pigou tax (applied of course to her income) is $t_2^{Ph} > 0$, and the male earner has $t_1^{Ph} < 0$. The intuition is clear: the planner wants to improve 2's position in the household and so imposes a tax to reduce her labour supply and increase her leisure, and thus her utility, and conversely for the primary earner 1.

Next, suppose that wage rates are not verifiably observable, so we must impose the *IC* constraints. Given the perfect matching assumption, the screening problem is unidimensional and there is a top household type H for which there is no distortion on incentive grounds, for the usual reason. In this case the paper shows that the optimal tax rates on earnings for household H are given by:

$$t_i^{EH} = \kappa_i t_i^{PH} \quad i,j = 1,2, \tag{76}$$

where

$$\kappa_i \equiv \frac{\phi_H/\alpha_i^H}{\phi_H/\alpha_i^H + \sum_{h<H} \mu_{Hh}} \in (0,1) \quad i = 1,2, \tag{77}$$

and μ_{Hh} are the multipliers on the downward binding constraints, at least one of which will be strictly positive. Thus the directions of distortions for this household type will be, because of the Pigou tax, just as in the case of symmetric information.

Finally, we have the case of households $h < H$. Here, for the tax rates on these households we have:

$$t_i^{Eh} \lesseqgtr 0 \text{ as } \kappa_i^h - \frac{\phi_h}{\alpha_i^h} t_i^{Ph} \gtreqless 0 \ \forall h < H, \ i = 1,2 \tag{78}$$

where $\kappa_i^h \gtreqless 0$ is a complex expression that depends in part on terms such as individual consumptions (that may not be observable), and that determine the sign of the expression representing the component of the tax relating to the Mirrlees incentive problem. Its sign and numerical value depend on the sum of the values of the multipliers on the binding *IC* constraints, the values of all

---

[31] Though strictly speaking, under symmetric information the planner is able to implement pure non-distortionary lump sum taxes. But here the Element is simply providing a benchmark case for the second best analysis.

the α_i^h-weights in the households corresponding to these binding constraints, and the slopes of their indifference curves at the optimal point. This expression was already encountered in Cremer et al. (2012) and extensively discussed there. The paper provides some special cases and numerical examples suggesting that the case in which $t_1^{Eh} < 0, t_2^{Eh} > 0$, that is a subsidy for the male partner and a tax for the female, is possible, though not assured. Thus the authors conclude:

> The main lesson that emerges from our paper is that the traditional Boskin and Sheshinski (1983) result calling for a lower marginal tax on the female spouse appears to be seriously challenged by the departure from a unitary couple model towards a bargaining setting. While the results are often ambiguous, it is clear that it takes rather rigorous conditions to obtain a lower marginal tax rate for the female spouse.

The comparison of the results of the tax model in this paper with those of Boskin and Sheshinski however requires more careful discussion, as does the household model from which the conclusion that the planner will want to reduce the female and increase the male labour supply essentially stems.

On the first point, care should be taken in comparing results obtained from very different tax models. As we have demonstrated, the Boskin/Sheshinski result arises from two stylised facts in a linear taxation model: that women have higher labour supply elasticities than men and the tax rate on women is a less powerful redistributive instrument than a tax on men. It is true that replacing the unitary household model by the collective model used by Cremer et al. would, in the Boskin/Sheshinski analysis, have a tendency to raise the female tax rate, and for the same reason. However, we question the basis for the Cremer et al. result, which is the assumption that women are supplying more labour to the market than the utilitarian planner would like, therefore it is in their interests if we use the tax system to discourage that.

Before we discuss this more fully, we also make the general point that we should be very cautious about applying theoretical results derived in the setting of a Mirrlees optimal tax model to any real-world existing tax system. A Mirrlees tax system requires type-dependent taxes that fully separate all types in the set of households under consideration. Real tax systems instead embody a great deal of pooling of heterogeneous types, as we pointed out in the previous section. Moreover, in a Mirrlees model marginal tax rates are designed to guide choices in such a way as to achieve this separating equilibrium, and, given these tax rates, type-specific lump sums are paid to achieve distributional goals. In real tax systems, lump sum transfers may be made to groups that can be tagged, but marginal tax rates are also important instruments for distributional purposes.

The assumption on which these results are based follows from a model that excludes household production as a form of time use for women as second earners. The intuition is simple: if women have lower bargaining power then a reduction in their net wage[32] can result in their receiving lower consumption of both leisure and market goods as well as fewer hours spent in market labour supply, but with more time spent in the production of household goods. The policy of increasing the tax on women and reducing that on men will reduce the opportunity cost of household production, as well as reducing female bargaining power. Given that household goods are normal goods the household's demand for them will increase, and this will induce a switch of the women's labour supply from the market to household production, as well as worsening the inequality within the household. The result may then be to make women as second earners even less well off. Certainly it does not make them unambiguously better off, as the Cremer et al. paper assumes. Finally, it is worth noting that governments have other instruments than income tax rates to influence the within-household welfare distribution, such as rules on the division of property at divorce or the tagging of specific household members as the recipients of transfer payments.[33] At the very least such instruments should be taken account of in the analysis.

5 Conclusions

In this Element we have sought to provide an in-depth survey of the papers written on the optimal taxation of the incomes of the members of family households, over the period beginning with the early 1980s and ending in the late 2010s. This literature, solidly within the public finance tradition, is not large, and so we have chosen to give fairly full exposition and discussion of the main contributions. We have not mentioned empirical and macroeconomic work in this area, except where the results are directly relevant to some elements of the theory.

We have classified the papers according to the type of tax system they have dealt with: linear, piecewise linear and non-linear taxation. A further distinction arises between models that do or do not take account of differences in preferences for consumption and labour supply of the household members and the effects of taxation on the within-household distribution of well-being. Those

---

[32] Studies in family economics on the effects of wage rates on within-household inequality typically ignore tax rates and work in terms of gross wage rates. For an important exception see Bick et al. (2018).

[33] See Lundberg et al. (1997), for example.

that do are very much in the minority, though the most recent work is tending to take that direction, particularly that in family economics more generally.[34]

It will perhaps be unsurprising that our own preferred approach to theoretical work in this area is to adopt the piecewise linear tax system as the basis for the analysis. This is not only because the theoretical results of the analysis, as we have discussed them in Section 3, can be derived without having to sprecify any particular household model, since the results in terms of sufficient statistics do not depend on them. We just have to accept the standard assumptions about the properties of the relationships between indirect utility functions and constraint functions on the one hand, and the tax instruments on the other. This is far from being the case for non-linear taxation in general, as we have seen in Section 4. Of course, the specific forms of those indirect utility functions and constraint functions play a crucial role in the interpretation and empirical application of those results. More importantly however, since piecewise linear tax systems are almost exclusively the type of tax system that exists in reality, this implies greater relevance and applicabilty to real-world tax problems. We are well aware that many of our colleagues working in this area would not agree with us on this point.

---

[34] See in particular Browning and Gørtz (2012) Cherchye et al. (2012), Gayle and Shephard (2019), and Lise and Yamada (2019).

References

Andrienko, Y., Apps, P., & Rees, R. (2016). Optimal taxation and top incomes. *International Tax and Public Finance*, 23(6): 981–1003.

Apps, P., Long, N. V., & Rees, R. (2014). Optimal piecewise linear income taxation. *Journal of Public Economic Theory*, 16(4): 523–545.

Apps, P., & Rees, R. (1988). Taxation and the household. *Journal of Public Economics*, 35(3): 355–369.

Apps, P., & Rees, R. (1999). Individual vs joint taxation in models with household production. *Journal of Political Economy*, 107(2): 393–403.

Apps, P., & Rees, R. (2009). *Public Economics and the Household.* Cambridge: Cambridge University Press.

Apps, P., & Rees, R. (2018). Optimal family taxation and income inequality. *International Tax and Public Finance*, 25(5): 1093–1128.

Apps, P., & Rees, R. (2022). Inequality measurement and tax/transfer policy. *International Tax and Public Finance*, 29: 953–984.

Atkinson, A., & Stiglitz, J. (1976). The design of tax structures. *Journal of Public Economics*, 6(1–2): 55–75.

Bick, A., & Fuchs-Schündeln, N. (2018). Taxation and labor supply of couples across countries: A macroeconomic analysis. *Review of Economic Studies*, 85(3): 1543–1576.

Boadway, R. (1988). The Mirrlees approach to the theory of economic policy. *International Tax and Public Policy*, 5: 67–81.

Boskin, M., & Sheshinski, M. (1983). Optimal tax treatment of the family: Married couples. *Journal of Public Economics*, 20(3): 281–297.

Brett, C. (2007). Optimal nonlinear taxes for families. *International Tax and Public Policy*, 14: 225–261.

Browning, M., & Gørtz, M. (2012). Spending time and money within the household. *Scandinavian Journal of Economics*, 114: 681–704.

Cherchye, L., De Bock, B., & Vermeulen, F. (2012). Married with children: A collective labor supply model with detailed time use and intrahousehold expenditure information. *American Economic Review*, 102(7): 3377–3405.

Chetty, R. (2009). Sufficient statistics for welfare analysis: A bridge between structural and reduced-form methods. *Annual Review of Economics*, 1: 451–488.

Cremer, H., Lozachmeur, J.-M., Mortando, D., & Roeder, K. (2016). Household: Bargaining and the design of couples taxation. *European Economic Review*, 89: 454–470.

Cremer, H., Lozachmeur, J.-M., & Pestieau, P. (2012). Income taxation of couples and the tax unit choice. *Journal of Population Economics*, 25: 763–788.

Gayle, G.-L., & Shephard, A. (2019). Optimal taxation, marriage, home production and family labor supply. *Econometrica*, 87(1): 291–326.

Immervoll, H., Kleven, H., Kreiner, C., & Verdelin N. (2011). Optimal tax and transfers for couples with extensive labour supply responses. *Journal of Public Economics*, 95(1): 485–500.

Kleven, H., Kreiner, C., & Saez, E. (2009). The optimal income taxation of couples. *Econometrica*, 77(2): 537–560.

Lise, J., & Seitz, S. (2011). Consumption inequality and intra-household allocations. *Review of Economic Studies*, 78: 328–355.

Lise, J., & Yamada, K. (2019). Household sharing and commitment: Evidence from panel data on individual expenditures and time use. *Review of Economic Studies*, 86: 2184–2219.

Lundberg, S., Pollak, R., & Wales, T. J. (1997). Do husbands and wives pool resources? Evidence from the United Kingdom child benefit. *Journal of Human Resources*, 32: 463–480.

McClelland, R., Mok, S., & Pierce, K. (2014). Labor force participation elasticities of women and secondary earners within married couples. *Working Paper 2014–06. Congressional Budget Office.*

Mirrlees, J. (1971). An exploration in the theory of optimum Income taxation. *Review of Economic Studies*, 38: 175–208.

Mirrlees, J. (1976). Optimal tax theory. *Review of Economic Studies*, 38: 175–208.

Pechman, J. (1977) (ed). *Comprensive Income Taxation*. Washington, DC: Brookings Institution.

Rosen, H. (1976). Is it time to abandon joint filing? *National Tax Journal*, 30: 423–428.

Saez, E. (2002). Optimal income and tax transfer programmes. *Quarterly Journal of Economics*, 117(2): 1039–1072.

Samuelson, P. (1956). Social indifference curves. *Quarterly Journal of Economics*, 70: 1–22.

Schroyen, F. (2003). Redistributive taxation and the household: The case of individual filings. *Journal of Public Economics*, 87(11): 2527–2547.

Sheshinski, E. (1972). The optimal linear income tax. *Review of Economic Studies*, 39: 297–302.

Slemrod, J., Yitzhaki, S., Mayshar, J., & Lundholm, M. (1994). The optimal two-bracket linear income tax. *Journal of Public Economics*, 53(2): 269–290.

For EU product safety concerns, contact us at Calle de José Abascal, 56–1°,
28003 Madrid, Spain or eugpsr@cambridge.org.

www.ingramcontent.com/pod-product-compliance
Ingram Content Group UK Ltd.
Pitfield, Milton Keynes, MK11 3LW, UK
UKHW020852180525
458533UK00014B/214